YOUR
CHURNING
PLACE

G/L
REGAL
BOOKS ™

A Division of G/L Publications
Glendale, California, U.S.A.

Robert L. Wise

Other good Regal reading:
Do I Have to Be Me?, Lloyd H. Ahlem
Caring Enough to Confront, David Augsburger
Dr. James Dobson Talks About Anger
Dr. James Dobson Talks About God's Will
Dr. James Dobson Talks About Guilt
Dr. James Dobson Talks About Love

Scripture quotations in this publication are from the
following versions:
Phillips, The New Testament in Modern English,
Revised Edition, J.B. Phillips, Translator.
© J.B. Phillips 1958, 1960, 1972. Used by permission of
Macmillan Publishing Co., Inc.
RSV, Revised Standard Version of the Bible,
copyrighted 1946 and 1952 by the Division of
Christian Education of the NCCC, U.S.A., and used
by permission.

Second Printing, 1978

Published by Regal Books Division, G/L Publications
Glendale, California 91209
Printed in U.S.A.

Library of Congress Catalog Card No. 76-53379
ISBN 0-8307-0510-4

To Barbara
Todd, Tony, Tate, Traci
without whom I could
not be complete.

CONTENTS

Foreword **7**

Preface **9**

1 The Gift of Personal Wholeness **13**

2 Guilt—the Avenger **23**

3 Self-Centeredness—the Ego and I **39**

4 Escapism—Checking Out **59**

5 Change—the Hooded Bandit **75**

6 Jealousy—the Green-Eyed Monster **91**

7 Anxiety—the Gnawing Devourer **107**

8 A Final Kiss from Christ **123**

A study guide for group or personal
use is available for this book.

FOREWORD

There is a churning place in all of us. Since childhood, mine has been in the pit of my stomach.

I wish that Robert Wise would have written this book twenty years ago and that I could have had a chance to read it then.

Dr. Robert Wise is not only very compassionate and sensitive to human needs, he is very practical and spiritual in his approach to the emotional problems of human life.

I *know* that his suggestions work—at least, they work for me!

I hope and pray that many of God's children will find a new completeness through the reading of this book, and I thank God for HIS wisdom that shines out in every page.

—Hansi
Maria Anne Hirschmann

PREFACE

Everyone has a churning place!

You discover it in the early years of your life. It seems to be located either near the pit of your stomach or at the base of your neck, where every muscle tightens. When it begins to turn and pump like an old washing machine, you find that every other area of your life marches to its lumbering, dull, paralyzing beat.

Ghosts and monsters engaged my childhood churning machine. Misgivings and a sense of inadequacy lurked behind those symbols that hid in that place of pressure. Do you remember what it was like for you?

Adolescence only increases the beat. New fears about "making it" with other people usually emerge along with the first acne, and the fears are just as infecting as the pimples!

9

"How can I be so ugly in such a world of beautiful people? Why should I be so dumb with so many smart people everywhere?" On and on it goes. In the teen years the churning place seems to work overtime. No one seems to escape its fierce action.

In adulthood our needs only become more sophisticated. The problems loom larger and the consequences appear more final. Yet we have the same churning place we discovered at age four. Now, however, the ghosts are real people who are quite willing to betray our confidences and manipulate our decisions. All the insecurities of love and money seem to give an endless prospect to the churning. At times it appears that the agonies will be eternal in duration! Dreams fail and hopes are lost. How well we now know the exact location of our churning place!

Believer or infidel, it is all the same. Nothing exempts us from the relentless process created by haunting memories and bankrupt expectancies. As universal as the human heart and head, the existence of the churning place cannot be denied.

And it is not a constructive place. Positive thoughts lead to action and results, but the churning place is a tank that fills with anxieties that just settle into stagnant infection.

The following pages are written in quest of a vaccine to counteract the effects of this reservoir of illness. Through the years I have found various sedatives, remedies, and antidotes that have cooled and soothed. Ideas and insights have changed my way of responding to life's disappointments and difficulties. This book has afforded me the opportunity of sorting out these discoveries and applying them to some of the major causes that create the churning place in our lives.

Much of the impetus for writing came from a conver-

10

sation at the conclusion of one particular counseling session. Though the session occurred a number of years ago and seemed minor at the time, the discussion left me with a haunting question. After discussing her current problems, the young divorcee asked me pointedly, "But does anybody ever *really* get changed because they believe in Jesus Christ?"

Sunday preaching was OK. Sure, the church had to put out its propaganda. That was fine with the ex-wife. But with all these problems buried deep within her life, was it truly possible that the Christian faith could change anything? Are there *really* spiritual answers to emotional problems?

Since that afternoon I have been striving to find and clarify these practical possibilities in the Christian faith. I want to be able to express them at the point of human need. Yes, people are truly changed by their faith! The following pages will zero in on how this actually can happen to you.

Churning places can become *turning* places. The problems that plague us are actually some of God's best opportunities to enter our lives in a dramatic way. Emotional circumstances usually keep us from seeing spiritual possibilities, but once we understand this fact, those centers of turmoil can be changed into quiet places.

This book is written with the promise that this peace can be your experience! It is my conviction that the answer you need may be only a few pages away. I believe it because the following insights have come straight out of life itself.

I have tested each of these ideas in the laboratory of the counseling office. From watching the results, I know how the sensitive centers of conflict can be changed. Much more, I have tested these ideas in my own life.

Believe me, I don't plan to preach at you. I just want

to share what I've seen and what I know faith will accomplish for you. If you experience freedom from your churning place, I'd be delighted to know about it. Although books aren't usually part of a dialogue, in this case I'd like to get your response.

In addition, I am grateful to three key people whose encouragement led me to try my hand at a book. A number of years ago Keith Miller challenged me to consider writing. At the time I couldn't believe it would be possible, but I began to follow one of his suggestions. Keith shared the value of keeping a journal, so I began to write down what was happening to me emotionally, and the discoveries I was making. Much of this material has come from the daily diary of my spiritual pilgrimage.

Second, my dear sister in Christ, Maria Anne Hirschmann (known to many readers as "Hansi") further encouraged me to write. With her keen and kind instruction I have tried to learn something of the rules of journalism. I am grateful for her hours in reading and in helping me prepare this manuscript. But most of all, her faith in my abilities encouraged me to try something that didn't seem possible.

Finally, Fritz Ridenour completed giving me the vision of making a book happen. His patient encouragement and confidence have meant much!

Without the faithful, diligent work of Dorothy Waltz, the typing and corrections wouldn't have been done. Faithful friends are one of God's best gifts to remedy the churning place!

Robert L. Wise
Laguna Hills, California
June 20, 1976

1
THE GIFT
OF PERSONAL
WHOLENESS

When she entered the office her face looked tense and drawn. As she sat down to explain her reason for coming, she had tears in her eyes. The same tense, beaten look that I had felt the first time I met her was draped around her movements like a mantle of anguish. She clutched at a handkerchief as she told a story of being haunted by frustration and anxiety.

"Everywhere I turn I drag a cloud of depression. I can't shake these nagging doubts and hopeless dreads. I'm not sure life is worth living anymore."

This lady's emotions were more twisted than the handkerchief she held so tightly in her hand. During the next several weeks this troubled woman shared the story of her miserable childhood that she simply couldn't forget. At every point her past erupted like a volcano of mental infection. Together we tried to peel back her experience. Layer by layer emerged a story of a childhood filled with abuse and rejection. She had not known what it meant to feel acceptance. The indelible imprint of loneliness marked her every hope.

That afternoon it all broke loose. Down at the bottom of her ominous depression lurked the unspeakable reason for these problems. She released it with a vengeance.

"I hate my father! I have hated him for years. I can't get rid of the thought. I try not to think about it. I put it out of my mind, but it seems to hide behind my every feeling. I hate him!"

As we talked, her hostility gave way to understanding. It was not long before she saw her real need to forgive her father. As her heart released the past, the deep roots of depression dried up. A new woman gradually emerged. In our last session she summarized the change:

"The little child in me has been touched by the finger of Jesus. He has reached right through the years and lifted my troubled center. For years I churned inside, but now my life is so calm!"

You have the same possibility for experiencing that healing touch! You might feel that this is only for others. That's not true! If you are open, you will not only find a pathway out of your many concerns, but your deepest problems will be turned into a new promise. Today's thorns can be tomorrow's roses in your life. Such great changes are not only for a few select, "special" people. They are meant for everyone; they are meant for *your* condition.

Again and again every minister sees frightened, desperate people who are seeking healing of past memories and present pain. Our time is particularly troubled with external tensions and internal emotional demands that are more pressing than most of us can comfortably bear. We are overpowered by traumatic experiences that rip out our vitality. If many of your problems seem more than you can bear, don't feel that you are a peculiarity—you are with today's vast majority!

But here's the good news: There is help for the child of your past, and there is an answer for your needs of the present. Nothing is as exciting as the opportunity of faith. I want to share with you the way to this discovery. Your problems and circumstances need not have the last word in your life.

The key word is *salvation*. Perhaps you've heard this term used only in a very religious, churchy way. Maybe it sounds like the least helpful suggestion I could offer. But salvation is exactly what happened to that woman who had hated her father since childhood.

The Greek origin of the word "salvation" means "wholeness" and it implies a *total* healing in every aspect of our lives. The Christian faith holds out to you and me the promise of that completeness. Salvation is the gift of personal wholeness.

The Lost Message

The great message of personal wholeness has been lost in recent decades because the Christian life has been narrowed down to trying to do the right things. This narrowness has been proclaimed as moralism. Many people have tried so hard to be correct! At the same time most people have been afraid to admit that "believing" only adds to the burdens they already carry within them. Sincere people have been devoutly trying to be "good" Christians. The center of their Christian experience has been mostly "trying," "doing," and "keeping good appearances," with the final hope of ending up almost as perfect as Jesus.

Many troubled persons have wondered if becoming as good as most Christians try to appear is the answer. They suspect they just don't have it within themselves to be that correct! So they give the whole thing up and shrug their shoulders: "Too bad some people are just better than others and born to be saints. I guess I'll always be in the 'out' group."

How tragic! Both within and without the church, people with this perspective can't help but carry overwhelming spiritual burdens. Certainly they are not experiencing the promised healing and wholeness the Bible extends to everyone. The Good News is gone!

But today we are beginning to grasp the fact that salvation is not *doing*, but coming to a new sense of being. The goal of our lives is not just to *feel better* but to *really be better* because a new man is emerging. Christianity is not something we *do* but something we *are*. It isn't a new method of trying harder, it's a living product of what God Himself has begun to do in and for us. It is finding the secret of opening ourselves to the marvelous power for change that is available in and through Jesus Christ. That's a whole new ball game!

This book is written to tell you in practical terms how this message can make your life whole. My one goal is to help you find this changed life. If you are afflicted with an agonizing problem right now, don't despair! It is my conviction that every one of us can find a promised personal wholeness beyond what we have ever dreamed possible. Guilt, egotism, escapism, fear, jealousy, anxiety—all are covered by this claim. There is no emotional need that is beyond the reach of this new sense of being.

God is waiting to give you His wholeness, and I am

writing this book to help you find it. I know it's possible!

The Secret That Found Me

My conviction is born from personal discovery. Though it wasn't easy, it has reshaped my life. When I left college I was an agnostic humanist. My struggles with life, faith, and human need had occurred in a critical environment that left me with the conclusion that theology and the Bible didn't have much to offer anybody. The humanities and social sciences seemed to be the new hope. I did want to help people, and the most practical door seemed to be social work.

Social work engages human hurting head-on, so I put on my helmet to do battle. With the "new answers for the new age" as my sword and shield, I had total confidence that emotional brokenness could be quickly mended. But even more quickly I discovered that the dragons of loneliness, despair, and cruelty yield easily to no man!

My battleground was set by a particular perimeter. My social work premise was the concept that the key to improving the world and its people is found in *changing the external environment.* If we change something about the social setting, I thought, then the person himself will be able to change, and his recovery is on the way. Many people hope for this same solution for their personal problems.

How often have you heard this conversation? "I would by happy if only I had the right job. I would be happy if I just had the right wife. Just a little more income or a new car would fix things up."

So the social worker's battlefield is working to get things right at schools, helping to supply funds, or finding foster homes. If we can just rearrange some outside dimension of life, then things on the inside will be great!

17

However, I soon found out that it doesn't work that way! Changing the *externals* doesn't necessarily affect the *internal* person at all. I was haunted by the fact that, in so many instances, after a better situation was provided we still had unhappy, disturbed, distressed people on our hands. Though I was helping people *externally*, they couldn't seem to find any final sense of happiness and fulfillment in life!

Then a new idea grasped me If something could really be changed *internally*, then the externals would take care of themselves! My strategy was just the reverse of what it should have been. In retrospect that seems awfully simple to understand, and perhaps even trite. Yet countless millions live their lives on the external basis. In fact, most American advertising thrives on that empty premise.

Eventually I became really intrigued with the idea of finding a way to help people change inside, so they could make the world on the outside a better place in which to live. Here is where the secret found me! As out of a fog I started to realize that Christian people really had the key to changing the total person. I knew of some Christians who had found the answer to their basic orientation to life, and were experiencing lives that were forever different.

Their explanation was that Jesus Christ is the key to all permanent change. They proclaimed by their lives that this ancient Man from Galilee is still alive and is at work *internally* right now! The secret is that through Him we can discover everything that is necessary for our personal wholeness and emotional completeness. He changes motivation by working at the center of our being. What an exciting thought! What an amazing message!

Out of this came another discovery. As I began to

rethink those earlier conclusions about theology and the Bible, something new leaped out at me—good theology contains a form of psychology! Locked up in all those big theological words and phrases is insight into the secret of what makes people do what they do! Theology wants to show us how to be emotionally sound. The Ten Commandments, the Beatitudes, the Lord's Prayer, etc., all have sets of keys that open the closed doors to self-actualization. I discovered that what Christianity teaches and what Christians believe are not just ideas to be debated, but paths to ultimate reality!

You Can Find Absolute Reality

One of the goals of therapeutic psychology is to help people discover reality. People sometimes get lost in their experiences and lose the ability to know what is true and false. Therapy helps to sort out these illusions and worn-out personal images. A person becomes free to live by learning the truth about himself.

I was astonished to discover that theology shares this same goal! When the Bible talks about the eternal, it is proclaiming final reality that will never change. It lifts up a picture of what man is intended to be. Illusions and images can be tested and corrected around these norms. Through the centuries, theology has helped establish sound mental health by pointing people beyond personal deception and leading them to authentic self-discovery.

But there is one important difference: Contemporary psychotherapy doesn't claim to give you a final grip on reality. It can only tell you what is *relatively* true about yourself. Though psychotherapy can help you sort out antiquated self-preconceptions, it cannot leave you with final conclusions that will give you absolute direction. This leaves you with a real problem. This topsy-turvy

19

world is constantly changing the rules on us, so after you get your head on straight, where do you *really* go from there?

Christian theology is just the opposite! It clarifies illusion in order to give direction. It defogs our images to create a new shape to our personhood. The Christian description of reality is final and absolute. You can bet your life on it, knowing that the result will be personal wholeness.

Here was a whole new way to help people! I wondered if I could study the disciplines of both theology and psychology to uncover more positive direction for life. Leaving behind the old "do-it-yourself morality" of yesteryear, I found that faith *really could* make sense for troubled people. Christian teaching was broader than I had ever dreamed!

Clearly, what I am sharing are not just academic discoveries. Some very personal and moving results began to change my own frustrations and fears. We all have problems, and I expect to have them to the day I die, but something marvelous and transforming began to happen to my problems through these new insights. I began to experience everything that was being promised in the Bible.

For example, having been an adopted child, I was always plagued by a poor sense of identity. Throughout most of my childhood and adolescence I struggled with problems of depression. Amazingly, the Christian insights that came from an encounter with Jesus Christ were healing these hidden aches. A whole new orientation to life began within me. With it came terrific release from fears, doubts and pressures that had undermined my sense of self-confidence and personal worth. Burdens that I had never even recognized as being present disappeared. When they left, I recognized what a detriment they had been! A new sense of belonging and well-being settled over my troubled life. I could breathe easily and freely. It was all right for me to be in this world after all! How good to be alive!

Old Emotions in New Pants

Two emotions gradually took on a new dimension in my life. First, love became a real possibility. I had been a very egotistical person, always trying to manipulate the world around my own needs. But now I found I could regard other people's needs as being as important as my own. From this I experienced a second phenomenon—a joy that at times flooded over every irritant like the tide covering the rough sand of the beach. As the happiness flowed out, everything was left smooth and in its proper place.

Once I walked down a hall in an empty building and felt an urge to just "kick up my heels." I began to run down the hall, leaping every few steps and clicking my heels together in the air. With childish glee I ran through the empty halls full of joy like a little child. I remember thinking, "I'm alive, I'm well, I'm happy, I'm free— thank God I'm free!" Out of breath, I stopped and leaned against a wall and thought how crazy this would look—a grown man running, laughing, and panting for no reason except that he was happy to be alive! If this is insanity, I absolutely prefer it to the kind of sanity with which I lived my life before that time.

My expressions of joy were anything but academic discoveries, and I know they can happen to you. And then came another strange discovery. As I studied the truth of the Christian faith, I discovered that something powerful was being added to my life. And then I discovered that this "something" is actually a new dimension that works within me. This new power not only helped me to see the world better, but it also helped me to understand what I was learning. Later I was to discover that this power is actually the divine Person of the Holy Spirit.

The Holy Spirit is really in my life, helping me to change and changing me at the same time. This means that a "new being" really is possible. This is *not* something I do myself. It is not even something I *could* do if I wanted to. The Holy Spirit's power is purely a gift, the gift of the good life. The most amazing thing of all is that God the Father wants to give us this gift even more than we want to receive it!

When we understand this, Christian doctrine becomes very practical. It becomes the key to change and to reality itself. When we appropriate Christian faith psychologically, it becomes a life changer! In the following chapters I will talk about six areas that are the most basic and demanding in my life and the lives of people I have sought to help. These six emotional problem areas are:

- guilt
- egotism
- escapism
- change
- jealousy
- anxiety

My goal is to apply the teachings of the Christian faith to each of these problems in a practical way. I believe it is possible to get rid of the ghosts that haunt our lives. I know, from studying Christ's promises and from personal experience, that His hand can reach and calm your churning place.

2
GUILT
THE AVENGER

According to Plutarch, a Greek biographer and philosopher, Vivides was a popular dramatic poet who lived six centuries before Christ. (Today's historians agree that Vivides was a very important figure in ancient Greek society.) One day as Vivides traveled from Corinth to Athens, he was accosted by two men who beat him, robbed him, and were about to kill him. Suddenly Vivides looked up in the sky and saw a flock of cranes overhead. With his last breath of life he cried out for the cranes to avenge him, and then he gasped and died.

The authorities made a lengthy investigation. All Greece cried out for revenge, since with its small city-states everyone knew of Vivides' murder. Unfortunately, there were no clues. Would this tragic murder go unsolved? Would the murderers get away without undergoing proper justice? The people of Corinth pondered the crime in a quandary.

Eventually they decided to call on the avenging furies to come forth. They began a dramatic, exciting, massive drama to bring forth vengeance from across the country. The people gathered in the outdoor amphitheater, and on the stage they acted out the call for vengeance for this great crime. The actors wore strange, Medusa-like hats, and snakes were flying in every direction. Greater and greater anticipation built as the actors called for vengeance and justice. Suddenly, as the fates would have it, a whole flock of cranes flew overhead. At the very climax of the play, while the cranes were flying overhead, a man in the audience jumped up and cried, "Comrade, the avenging cranes of Vivides have come for us!" Instantly the people knew that these two men were the murderers. They seized them, and execution soon followed.[1]

Plutarch penned this story in order to tell people how guilt will inescapably be discovered. As the people of Corinth dramatized outwardly what was happening inwardly in the lives of the murderers, the drama finally convicted the murderers.

In a sense you and I are just like that. At various times all of us have guilt which can't be eluded. Sooner or later that guilt comes back overhead like those flying cranes, and we find ourselves trapped. Who hasn't experienced the phenomenon of gnawing, aching fear that the avenger, guilt, brings? All of us have suffered under it at one time or another.

The Avenger Cripples

I want to share from my counseling experiences how such emotions and feelings have plagued Christian people. As a social worker I had the opportunity to observe and study how these destructive dynamics develop. After becoming a pastor I observed these same

24

emotions playing havoc in the church. Nothing is more difficult to deal with than the problem of guilt.

Guilt is a primary problem that every minister sees day in and day out. Time and again people come to the office wanting to make confession in some way. They bring a problem that seems to be far removed from guilt, yet underneath there is the hidden struggle with guilt itself. It infects our relationships and makes us ill; it makes us paranoid and produces all kinds of spin-offs if it is not resolved. Let's look at a story from the Bible about the power of guilt.

Jesus and the Paralytic

Jesus was in Capernaum when a paralytic was brought in lying flat on a bed. When Jesus saw the faith of those who had brought in this man, He said to the cripple, "Cheer up, my son! your sins are forgiven." At once some of the scribes thought to themselves, "This man is blaspheming!" But Jesus said to them, "Why must you have such evil thoughts in your minds? Do you think it is easier to say, 'Your sins are forgiven' or 'Get up and walk'? But to make it quite plain that the Son of Man has full authority on earth to forgive sins ... 'Get up, pick up your bed and go home.' " And immediately this man sprang to his feet and went home. And the crowd was filled with awe and praised God for giving such power to men. (See Matt. 9:1-8, *Phillips.*)

Here a man comes in on a stretcher and the people look at his twisted body and say "paralysis." But Jesus looks beyond the man's physical handicap and says "guilt"! People would have said that this man needed therapy. But Jesus said that this man needed reconciliation with God. He recognized that the man's real problem was his guilt. In some inexplicable way this was tied to his paralysis.

25

This story demonstrates that health and happiness demand forgiveness of sins. You and I cannot become the full stature of the person we are intended to be without an ongoing sense of forgiveness in our lives. As a corollary, no man finds this freedom completely except as Christ touches his life. Let's think together about how this can happen and how we can defeat the avenger, guilt.

In the first place, guilt makes you sick. It is an inescapable fact that guilt will have repercussions throughout your entire body. Go through the New Testament and notice how Jesus looked at physical conditions and saw them as a need for reconciliation. Health came as He touched that point. In my own ministry I have seen the terrific power of guilt to make people sick. Guilt in a person is like a rocket shot off on the Fourth of July. It explodes with fragments and particles that fall into many other areas of our lives that we would not expect.

We get contaminated by our own sense of guilt. Have you ever had the problem of getting a thorn or a little piece of wood stuck in your skin? It goes unnoticed until you wake up one morning and have a festering sore. Your whole body wants to push this thing out in any way it can. Guilt is exactly like that! The particles of its debris lodge within us. They will fester until they are pushed out. So often the pushing urge ends by spilling over into our other relationships. We come to fear each other; we are afraid to look honestly into each other's eyes, and we become a little paranoid.

The way in which guilt infects our relationships was illustrated most graphically by an experience my wife had with our two boys when they were small. Todd and Tony are less than a year apart, and as they grew up they were much like twins. If you have ever raised two boys like this, you know how hard it is to figure out "who done it!" On one of these "who done it" occasions, Barbara got the boys together and was giving them the third degree. Naturally, both claimed to be innocent.

Suddenly it hit her! She said, "Well, I know who did it. We are not going to discuss this any further, because the boy who did it has a white feather on his head."

Todd immediately looked straight at Tony's head, and Tony grabbed for the feather! Try that on your children sometime! Because of his guilt, Tony just knew that his mother could see what he felt. In a much more serious way, we fear what cannot be seen and project it on others. The results make us sick.

Guilt and Illness

The tragic story of guilt goes even further, for guilt shrivels us and affects our physical health. Somewhere in the dim past I remember reading a psychiatric article on the effects of a sick conscience in producing many nervous disorders. The real roots of the nervous twitch, the morbid fear, and the crippling depression are often found in a disturbed, guilt-ridden recollection of the past. That's so true! A conscience that is shriveled and infected will spill over and have dramatic internal repercussions. These internal responses can in turn filter down into tissue, muscle, and bone, making us into sick or immobilized persons.

Today we live in an age of moral tension. I think the poet Auden, who described ours as an age of anxiety, was so right. All around us we can see the tension. I remember seeing a picture in *Life* magazine of a random group of people crossing the street in New York City. It captured an amazing mood. As you looked at these faces you saw an enormous anxiety etched on them. Everyday people walking down a common street looked as though they were being pressured to death!

27

A recent random sample of a similar group of people from this area indicated that an alarmingly high proportion (85 percent) demonstrated an immediate need for psychiatric help. The truth is that behind many, many of these conditions is a basic need for confession. Unless the sources of this anxiety are exposed and confessed and dealt with, we all will find ourselves faced with the same possibilities for physical illness.

Shakespeare, with his magnificent English prose, writes this into a line from Richard the Third. King Richard was a very devious man. In one scene he soliloquized about the condition of his life: "My conscience has a thousand several tales, and every tale condemns me for a villain. Perjury, perjury in the highest degree. Murder, murder in the direst degree. All these several sins, all used in such degree, all throng to the bar, all crying guilty, guilty! I shall despair."[2]

Wherever he turned, wherever he hid, King Richard's sins continually came back to haunt him. Accusation after accusation, "guilty, guilty, guilty," was the internal verdict.

Guilt is the same with us—it has the same destructive power. When the guilt goes unsatisfied, the life remains unwhole. The avenger will not be escaped. Every past accusation remains ever-present.

This wouldn't have been news to the psalmist, for he understood it a long time ago: "Blessed is he whose transgression is forgiven, whose sin is covered. Blessed is the man to whom the Lord imputes no iniquity.... When I declared not my sin, my body wasted away through my groaning all day long. For day and night thy hand was heavy upon me; my strength was dried up as by the heat of summer" (Ps. 32:1-4, *RSV*). David knew what it was like to harbor guilt. Whether lying on his bed or walking down the street, he felt like the scorching desert sun was reducing him to a deflated football. So he recognized what he must do. "I acknowledged my sin to thee, and I did not hide my iniquity; I said, 'I will confess my transgressions to the Lord;' then thou didst forgive the guilt of my sin" (Ps. 32:5, *RSV*). That was what was needed, for without confession there would only be continued deterioration.

The same is true in Matthew's story of the paralytic brought to Jesus. Jesus looks at him. The paralytic acknowledges the truth about his condition and the result is a cripple made whole!

Now let's not deduce from this that *all* physical illness is a product of guilt. We have lots of "bugs," illnesses, and metabolic problems that have nothing at all to do with guilt. But in this man's condition Jesus saw that the deeper, larger problem of guilt was the true source of his suffering.

Guilt comes in many different ways. Sometimes it is a false guilt, and sometimes through personal relationships people dump their own guilt on us and it becomes ours. But if we carry this guilt, its oppressive effects will be the same as if it were our own.

Often the problem would not affect others as much as it does us—they might be able to shake it off in a casual manner. Yet we can't; it stays to haunt us. Whatever bothers us is real, and we must bring this before Christ, just as they brought this man on the pallet. Unless we are forgiven, there is no hope for happiness or strength or health. We can't get the scourge of guilt out of our systems unless Christ ultimately touches you and me. So let's face it—in order to be whole I must recognize that guilt makes me sick.

Guilt and Confession

Guilt demands confession. Once we see a problem,

we move on to discover what we can do about it. Let us realize the power and the place of confession. Confession has its own antibiotic power to sink deep to the source of the infecting illnesses that guilt brings. Yesterday's mistakes can be cleansed by today's honesty. Confessions are a vaccine, keeping all the things of yesterday from lingering within us and spoiling us by staying on as old viruses of past diseases.

Let's face it! At various times I must get guilt out of my system. By making confession (and retribution if necessary), I am able to become free of the past.

Here's how the impact of this fact came to me. Actually, I stumbled onto it even before I became a Christian. The truth came from a very unlikely source—the lectures of one of the great psychologists living today, Dr. O. Hobart Mowrer.

Dr. Mowrer has been a monolithic figure in the science of psychology.[3] However, the year he was elected president of the American Psychology Association he was unable to attend the convention because he was confined in a hospital! For a number of years this brilliant man had been under psychoanalysis. He was a master of his discipline and yet this was the result! Now he had an even stronger reason to discover what caused these problems. As he looked at his personal progress, he found something very significant.

The system of Freudian therapy which Mowrer had been using was predicated on one basic idea—the concept that guilt is really a figment of your imagination. This school of thought taught that conscience must be removed as an active force in order for a person to become well. The whole therapy process had been trying to talk Mowrer out of feeling guilty, but the result was that he just deteriorated.

Painfully, Mowrer discovered that this idea and approach were wrong. Guilt is a reality, and the fact that it bothers our conscience is really a sign of health! You cannot try to talk guilt away without getting sick. What you must do instead is to face up to the source of guilt as a fact of life. Mowrer discovered that if your conscience bothers you, then you have done something wrong! Instead of trying to talk yourself out of it, you must deal with it. On the basis of this, not as a religious man but as a scientist, he went to the teachings of Jesus to discover how guilt could be resolved. From there he developed an approach called integrity therapy.

Principles for Dealing with Guilt

To apply these insights, Mowrer developed three principles. Notice that these principles reveal the basic dimensions of the gospel. The first principle for taking care of guilt is that "secrecy causes us troubles." It separates us from our feelings. Openness with a significant other is the road back to normality.

Second, because it is easy but self-defeating to wear a mask and not acknowledge who we are, we must learn to drop all pretenses. This is best done by confession.

Third, openness by itself is not enough. The guilty individual is under obligation to make restitution according to the transgressions within his life.

In amazing similarity with the teachings of Jesus, Dr. Mowrer evolved a whole new plan that has given him the most successful practice he has ever known! He has healed many, many people with these principles. His discovery is that you and I have to face up to our guilt! We have to deal with it! To rid ourselves of guilt we must recognize it and do whatever is indicated to make all things right.

One particular dimension of Mowrer's insight has particularly helped me. I find that it is not so hard to want to get right with God, but it is much harder for me to want to get right with someone else. So the real measure for my getting right with God is my intention to get right with my fellowman.

If you are going to resolve the thing that made you feel guilty, it is not enough to go to God and confess it; your real confession will be expressed as you are also willing to make things right with men! Does this sound threatening? Does this make you feel ill-at-ease? Of course it does! But these feelings indicate that you are in touch with your real emotions, and it is only at this point that you can get free. But it is at this very point that many people fail to act, and this is why they have not known personal release from guilt.

It will help you to discover that you cannot wait to do this until you feel like it! Feelings come after actions; effort precedes comfort. It is only *after the rectification* that you will find the joy. Does this surprise you? It certainly reverses the way we have often expected things to be. Yet this is a powerful truth. Release will come *after* the deed of forgiveness in most instances!

I have seen this again and again in my own life and ministry. For example, I remember one woman who had chronic depression. She was deeply depressed, to the point of being immobilized.

One day she confided to me, "I'll just confess this: I have always hated my mother. I was the last child and I was not wanted. She made it clear to me all my life that they did not want me, that they were stuck with me. I have always hated her for it!"

I asked, "Do you really mean it?"

"I confess this with great pain."

I suggested a form of restitution that Jesus Christ presented. She would need to forgive her mother! The look on her face was one of stark terror.

"I would never do that!"

I responded, "Then you will be sick to the day you die. You must absolutely forgive her and make the necessary restitution within yourself." I was anything but unsympathetic. I knew this forgiveness would be painfully difficult. Yet it could not be avoided.

Later, however, it all came into focus for her in an evening worship service of healing prayer. (In these services we would pray for the mental and physical problems of those in need.) On this particular evening this troubled woman was moved to forgive her mother. That night was the last time she knew chronic depression! Wholeness came as her mind's eye could see Jesus saying, "Cheer up, daughter, your sins are forgiven."

This is the power of the gospel! It comes before us with this message: "Cheer up! You don't have to carry it with you!" This is what James meant when he said, "Confess your sins to one another, and pray for one another, that you may be healed" (Jas. 5:16, *RSV*). It is in this framework that we can not only *forgive* but *forget!*

When Dr. Mowrer suggests a "significant other" that you can be open with, he means the same thing James did: "Confess your sins to one another." Let's give a qualifying word to this. It doesn't mean that we tell everybody everything. We can get into an awful lot of trouble doing that! We must be very selective; we must find a "significant other" whom we know is trustworthy and will hold what we say in the most tender confidence. Not everybody can do this. In fact *most people* can't. But when we find the right "other" and confess our sin in this way, something powerful happens!

Guilt makes you sick, and guilt requires confession. So in this undercurrent guilt always demands God. Whatever has happened in your life and whatever you

33

do to make it right, at some point you have to hear deep within you the voice of God saying, "You are forgiven." Everything else is secondary until you know deep within your soul that you are forgiven. Some of us put ourselves through a lot of things in order to finally hear these words. But however we come to this point, once we know our guilt is forgiven our lives become buoyant. Isn't that exciting? This can be the real you! If you put yourself in the right position, God will be waiting to welcome you with the embrace of liberation.

Two Kinds of Guilt

I've learned that there are really *two* kinds of guilt, and that we need to be clear on this in order to receive the fullness of God's forgiveness. So far in this book I've been speaking about *real* guilt. Real guilt is based on something you've actually done wrong. You know there is a time and a place where something happened. This "something" is what you need to confess. It is real; you were there.

However, there is also *existential* guilt. This is guilt that isn't tied to a specific event. It's the vague, unnamed, missed-the-mark quality about your life. It's a piece in the puzzle that has never quite come together in your life. During moments of reflection, deep within yourself you find a sense of inadequacy.

For example, such symptoms often come when you reach the top in your career but feel there isn't anything there. Or you get to the other side of the mountain, where you always knew the pasture would be greener, only to discover it isn't. You find within yourself that you don't do the thing you ought to do. Sometimes you don't even want to try! There is something deep and unsettling within you that tells you that the condition of your life is just not right.

The first type of guilt, real guilt, is a separation between you and somebody else. You can do something about it with confession and restitution. But the second type of guilt, existential guilt, is a separation between you and God, and there is nothing you can do about it! Does that sound frightening?

Most of us have been reared with the American attitude that by *doing* we can accomplish anything. If I exert enough effort I can correct anything wrong in my life. If I have enough psychology, enough education, or enough money, I can correct and improve any defect in my life. Sorry, you *cannot* do enough to settle existential guilt!

Once you see this, you will understand why it is so powerful to know that Jesus Christ is the answer. The answer does not lie in anything you can do; it lies in *what has already been done in Jesus Christ.* When we find ourselves completely broken and separated, then it is *in the Cross* that we have the final picture of what God has already done for us. We could never do this for ourselves.

We grasp this freedom by faith. It is purely by faith in Jesus Christ that I can stand up and know that it's OK with me. Jesus said, "But that you may know that the Son of man has authority on earth to forgive sins ... I say to you, 'rise, take up your bed and go home' " (Luke 5:24, *RSV*). Stand up and claim the forgiveness! I can really experience this as I look at the totality of my life and know that I am not sufficient. There is not anything in me that is totally enough!

It is at this point that I can find complete sufficiency in Christ and can experience His full forgiveness. If you have never really discovered this, if you have never even *heard* this, I want you to listen closely.

Let these words come up off the page as if they are

taking shape in your ears as well as through your eyes. Listen to the words of Christ as He says, "*Your* sins are forgiven. Your *sins* are forgiven. Your sins *are* forgiven. Your sins are *forgiven.*" You can stand up and be released!

My most graphic image of this release comes from the movie *Ben Hur.* Judah Ben Hur's life has been ruined; his sister and mother have been ravaged by leprosy. Judah finds himself at the feet of this unusual man who is being unjustly crucified. As the crucifixion continues, the skies become black and violent. The death of this humble man is near.

Ben Hur is transfixed by gazing into the eyes of this pure and forgiving face. As the clouds gather and the storm breaks, the dying one utters, "It is finished!"

The camera focuses on the crucified hand with the nail holding it to the wood. The rain begins to fall and wash the blood down out of the palm. The crimson stream runs down the side of His arm, becoming darker as it runs off His foot. The blood mingled with the rainwater washes clean the side of the cross.

The blood drops into a pool of water at the foot of the cross, and the camera follows this puddle as it flows into a stream, then a tributary. The crimson ribbon soon becomes a mighty river and flows to the ocean as the blood of Christ goes forth to all the nations.

At one turn the stream passes Ben Hur's sister and mother as they stand under a tree seeking shelter from the storm. When they reach out to touch the water, it happens—they are clean! The dead tissues drop away, and their terrible sores begin to fade. In sheer amazement, they watch the terror of months of disease dissolve in a few moments of cleansing from the blood of the cross. They are whole because the blood of Christ has touched even them!

This is the power of God to forgive everything in every way in every man's life. In your life the avengers are there; they occur without warning like a flock of cranes rising on the horizon. Yet you can do something about them if you are willing to make confession and restitution.

Perhaps you feel unworthy to have God do anything for you, thinking that His door of forgiveness should be shut. Know that this door is always held open by a nail-scarred hand. There is always room at the foot of the cross to find the complete healing of guilt. The healing is there; health and wholeness are still available!

Some Helps to Wholeness

Why not reach out for this wholeness right now? Perhaps you'd like to pause and talk with God about this. Just put your thoughts into any words that are natural for you. Maybe praying the words of this prayer would express what you are feeling:

> Our gracious, forgiving, heavenly Father, I do want to wade into that healing stream that flows from the foot of the cross. My life has accumulated the dirt of the world. It has worked its way under my skin and left me scarred and marred with the residue of guilt. I hunger to hear your voice saying, "Cheer up, your sins are forgiven." So I ask forgiveness and am fully ready to make any restitution that will make me one with you and with all the others in my life. Give me the absolution and the resolution for all things necessary to the acquisition of wholeness. In the name of the One with the nail-scarred hands.
>
> Amen.

For Further Consideration

1. How does my guilt "feel"? How might it unconsciously have an effect on my actions?
2. What are the hardest areas of guilt for me to face in my past? In my present?
3. What are some of the ways in which I might begin to take responsibility for my life?
4. Is it possible that making restitution could change how guilt is affecting my life? What do I need to do to fully realize this?
5. Read 1 John 1:9. Ask God to show and confirm to you that this forgiveness can truly be yours!

Footnotes

1. Andrew P. Peabody, *Plutarch on the Delay of the Divine Justice* (Boston: Little, Brown, and Co., 1885).
2. *Complete Works of Shakespeare in Eight Volumes*, Vol. V (New York: The Co-operative Publication Society).
3. O. Hobart Mowrer, *The New Group Therapy* (New York: Van Nostrand Reinhold Co., 1964).

3
SELF-CENTEREDNESS
THE EGO AND I

I can't think of self-centeredness without remembering one of the most unusual people I ever encountered. He was a walking personification of the problem! This man dressed with such finesse that from 100 yards you could see him coming. However, his clothing wasn't so important, since from 200 yards you could tell he was wearing the worst toupee you had ever seen!

He would always come up to a new person and say, "I'll bet you don't know I'm wearing a toupee." What you felt like saying was, "Yes, my dog has one just like it!" But inevitably you would say something like, "Oh, how interesting." And you hated yourself for saying it.

Wherever he went he called attention to himself. He made himself the focal point in the most totally obnoxious way possible. So when I think about the subject of the ego and I, this man's image comes to mind. He was self-centeredness in double knits!

Self-centeredness is at the heart of a story in the life of Jesus. As Jesus arrives at the home of Mary and Martha, Martha receives Him and her sister Mary enters. Immediately Mary sits down to listen to Christ's teachings, but Martha is distracted by getting supper ready.

Soon Martha demands of Jesus, "Lord, do you not care that my sister has left me to serve alone?" But Jesus responds, "Martha, Martha, you are anxious and troubled about many things; one thing is needful. Mary has chosen the good portion, which shall not be taken away from her." (See Luke 10:38-42, *RSV*.)

There's nothing wrong with being a good hostess; you can't fault Martha for wanting the good silverware out and the roast done on time! But that misses the point. Martha was so caught up in herself, in her pursuits and her strivings, that she missed the meaning of the whole occasion. So Jesus revealed it to her: "Your sister has chosen the good portion."

Let's explore this better portion that is always open to us through our Christian faith. From my counseling experience I have observed again and again how self-centeredness erodes relationships and undermines our best emotions. From the other side of the desk, I have watched many couples and individuals miss the better portion because they were trapped in their own egotism. With enormous reluctance I have found these subtle tentacles of self-preoccupation wrapping themselves around my own best visions and personal hopes. Certainly, egotism is one of the most persuasive of all emotional problems.

Narcissism Isn't a Flower!

Is it appropriate to call self-centeredness an emotional problem? Certainly, narcissism is a clinical problem, since it means to be in love with oneself in an excessive and abnormal way. But is it appropriate to speak of self-centeredness in the same way we would of guilt or anxiety? I am convinced it is! From counseling people

40

who are troubled in their marriages, with problems in their business, and with failures in their relationships, I know that it is completely possible to be so caught up in our own egotism that it becomes a disease. Egotism can produce emotions that rob us of our strength and our faith just as surely as guilt, anxiety, or depression. Self-centeredness and egotism will keep us from ever being fully happy; the person caught in this web is always grasping at life but never quite getting the substance of true joy.

Some years ago a famous British woman died by suicide. She left a note saying, "I have never loved anyone and I am miserable." So she took her own life—a final proof of how utterly destroying and destructive self-centeredness can be.

Again, like guilt, self-centeredness seeps into all our relationships and destroys them. It creates empty ambition and a need to reach an impossible level of attainment, and therefore we cannot find satisfaction. We can never seem to reach high enough, and we become apprehensive of criticism. Anything negative becomes almost unbearable; everything has to be perfect or it cannot be absorbed. Envy develops when anyone else succeeds.

Self-centered people feel they must be on center stage at all times, but life seems to be passing them by. They never get the proper recognition or proper rewards. Justice is never quite done to the self-centered person. The result is always emptiness.

For clinical analysis, a tape-recording was once made of a counseling session with such a person. As you listen to the self-centered mentality, it comes out "I, I, I, me, me, me." It is utterly boring to listen to it! You find yourself fidgeting and looking for the off button!

Let me share another case study. One day I counseled a lady who had everything possible. She had a good husband; she had reached a level of income with plenty; her children were almost on the edge of leaving home; and yet she found herself burdened with chronic boredom. Life to her had no thrill or meaning. As I listened to her describe her boredom, there came the familiar "me, me, me, me." The connection between the two problems is utterly obvious. Now let's transport this back into the biblical setting.

Jesus and the Poor Rich Man

The eighteenth chapter of Luke tells the story of a wealthy young man who seemingly enjoyed everything life had to offer. Yet he found himself with the vexing dilemma of boredom.

We usually expect this story to tell us about the love of money, but I find that it has much more to say than to expose a money problem. Let me share my paraphrase. Listen to it with your inner ear, searching for the meaning behind it all.

This young man comes to Jesus and says, "Good Teacher, what must I do to inherit eternal life?" Immediately Jesus responds, "Good—how is it that you are using that word? Don't call me good like that. It's only appropriate to call God good!" Jesus is saying in effect, "The only person as good as you think you are is God! Don't confuse me with that."

Jesus asks the young man, "What is it that the law says makes you good?" The young man quotes back to Him the Ten Commandments, and then adds, "And all these I have observed from my youth!"

Now think about that for a minute. If someone would ask you, "What kind of a Christian are you?", would you quote the Ten Commandments and then say, "I have lived every word of it all my life"? Of course not. You wouldn't want to be called an egomaniac.

This young man wasn't shy about saying, "I've done it all!" Jesus, however, looked beneath the surface of his life and said to him, "You lack one thing—go sell it all." And the young egotist went away sorrowing. (See Luke 18:18-24.)

The key to the story is in the phrase, "Sell it all." In these words Jesus cuts to the core of the problem of self-centeredness. His surprising answer has an amazing prescription for wholeness. But His answer is even more profound than it seems on the surface. So let's probe the meaning of his self-centeredness further.

Charles Kingsley once wrote, "If you want to be miserable, think about yourself and what you want, what you are like, what people ought to think about you, and you will be wretched."[1] It's true!

The rich young ruler came to Jesus and said, "Good Teacher." Behind these seemingly complimentary words, our Lord caught an entirely different intent. Perhaps, the clue was in the man's dress. In a sea of naked, poor people, this young man was distinctively rich. Clearly, the wealthy youth wanted to distinguish himself from the common crowd.

Or, the tone of his voice may have had that telltale inflection. Rather than just being polite, the "good" may have smacked of too much separateness. "Jesus, isn't it marvelous *we* are not as other men?"

The selfless inner ear of Jesus heard the thumping ego-beat of the man's deeper motivation. He would not let the arrogant youth put Him into the superior class reserved for "special people." In this private club of the upper crust, "good" was a synonym for exclusive.

Instantly, Jesus zeroed in on the egotism that was latent in his words. What might have been learned from the Master was crowded aside by the desire to be special.

How tempting it is to number ourselves among the elite! The desire to be special is always a source of self-centeredness. Yes, we really *do* want to believe we are among the "good people," don't we? To keep our perspective clear, Jesus holds up the goodness of God as a study in contrast.

One of the most deadly things that can happen in a church is to begin to see ourselves as the "good people," with the "bad people" out there. This attitude is very insidious; it creeps inside our motives and relationships; it sounds so good and seems to be so true. After all, aren't we supposed to be good people? Yet this "goodness" becomes a means by which we elevate ourselves above those "other sinners."

But this kind of inverted piety is its own trap! Besides being completely phony, it silently alienates the very people whose affirmation we seek. Though this young man attempted to find recognition from Jesus, his effort turned into a curve ball and he struck out. The sad thing is that in everyday life we are not usually told that we have missed; people just walk away, and we don't realize that the game is over. Self-centeredness is always surprised to find that the grandstands are empty, and it gropes to find out why.

The really liberating possibility comes from just the opposite end. Real freedom comes when *I know I am a sinner!* Sound surprising? Sure, but it's the greatest release in the world to know that this is true. What Jesus said to that young man was, "Don't kid youself, son; I read your motives. I read your game. You're aiming at the wrong target. Don't try to tell me how good you are. It's a fruitless trip."

By the way, if no one has told you lately, let me share something personal with you. You are a sinner! Sorry about that, but it's the truth. You have to know it to get life straight. I know that "sinner" is a word with lots of strange connotations. Many people don't really understand the meaning of sin in its biblical context.

Recognizing that you are a sinner doesn't mean that you must put yourself down as a bad person, with evil oozing from every pore. It doesn't mean you have a scarlet letter under your skin just waiting to surface. Nor does it mean that God is waiting somewhere behind a tree, ready to zap you with a thunderbolt.

Recognizing you are a sinner means that you must be realistic about your motives. All of us move to put ourselves in the center of the universe; we naturally manipulate everything to serve our purposes; we want what we want when we want it.

Furthermore, we will do almost anything to achieve that end. Most subtly we will do whatever is necessary to be first. This is what it means to be a sinner. Until we recognize this and learn to see the difference between the goodness we would like to see as ours and the truth of our own sinfulness, we are not able to see how complete is the liberation that Jesus brought us.

So many of us are trapped in our own "goodness," just as the rich young ruler was. Caught by his own egotism, he could not recognize the source of his real need. Jesus tried to help him, but he could not accept any help. His ego was too strong.

A Self Evaluator for Self-Centeredness

What is egotism and self-centeredness? Try to answer this in a personal way. This is one problem that we like to think we don't have. Our own degree of self-centeredness is one of the most difficult personal things to apprehend! You and I don't really believe we are self-centered; everybody else has the problem. When I described the tape recordings of the woman with I, I, I, and me, me, me, I bet you were thinking of your mother-in-law, a relative, a friend, a business associate, or someone else you knew. You were not thinking about yourself!

Let me share with you a checklist that is a good measurement of whether self-centeredness might be part of your life. Answer yes or no to these questions.

1. Are you easily offended by what other people say?
2. Do you turn and direct conversations so they focus on you and your interests?
3. Do you demand a lot of attention from others?
4. When you work with a group or a committee do you desire to serve or do you wish to dominate?
5. Do you subtly manipulate people and circumstances until you get "your way"?
6. Are you ill-at-ease when an honor goes to someone else?
7. How do you take unexpected interruptions? Do you consider them unfair intrusions on your time?
8. Are most of your life's details concerned with yourself?
9. How about lending? Does it bother you to share and lend what is clearly and personally yours?
10. Do you feel that life has singled you out for particular adversities or injustice?

If you find yourself answering yes to several of these questions, I'm talking to you. This is a good test of whether self-centeredness fits into your life.

Hey, wait a minute. Don't get smug because you answered no to some of these questions. We all will do almost anything to let ourselves off the hook. (By the way, that's a characteristic of self-centered people.) Think about it again.

This time picture a scale of from 1 to 10. Place your responses on an imaginary line that measures your egotism. "1" represents no tendency at all and "10" will indicate extreme self-preoccupation. If you're over the 50 percent mark for several of these questions, you still have the problem!

The Roots of Narcissism

Where does this self-love all start? How is it that these excesses happen? There are essentially two sources for narcissism—this inordinate self-centeredness—and both have many implications in the rearing of our children. Psychology tells us that at around three years of age we develop the ability to look beyond ourselves. We begin to learn the meaning of "others." We can learn to share and find joy in giving, or we do not discover this and find satisfaction only in taking.

I can still see Todd and Tony sharing cookies at ages three and two. It usually began with two-year-old Tony holding a cookie. Three-year-old Todd simply took it away from him and began eating it. While munching, he rather objectively listened to his little brother wail in sheer agony. Todd always felt sharing was such fun! Obviously we had to do something with his idea of sharing or he would never get the point!

A child that is pampered and indulged may never learn to share. He will almost always develop with a blind spot. Since he had not learned the joy of reaching out to others, at this early age the disease of self-centeredness may begin to rot his best intentions.

I came to realize this early in my Christian life, while I was still making a transition between social work and the professional ministry. We decided to try an experiment with our children in order to help them learn the joy of sharing. So we began to use our home as a base for a ministry of caring.

During the next five years we opened our doors to a

47

whole series of houseguests. Some came for a short time, while others stayed longer. Around 30 unwed mothers, a couple of missionaries, a couple of needy students, and several others came to stay as they had need. Their needs required our children to share in a very radical way. Sometimes a room would have to be shared and sometimes they would have to give up a bed and sleep together. Some guests were kind and thoughtful, while others were irritable and difficult. There was lots of give and take in understanding and being understood. On some occasions it was fun but many times it was demanding and unrewarding.

The children were right in the middle of it all, learning to share their things and their lives. We were convinced this would cause them to learn to be open and to look at others' needs as well as their own. I believe this experience will become especially valuable for Todd and Tony as they become adults. But in any case, it has been an attempt to attack one of the sources of excessive self-interest in our own family.

The other source of self-centeredness comes from the opposite end of life's spectrum. Here we find a child who is so deprived and has so little that out of self-defense he must learn to scratch for himself to survive. In material things and in love, his own satisfactions are within himself. This child learns that he must live by looking out only for his own good, and so he develops into a person who is unable to reach out to others. This is one of the most tragic results that poverty can have. This poverty of personhood builds lives on a foundation of fear and apprehension. Countless millions have lived and died with a daily gnawing of suspicion that forces existence to be lived only for survival.

Most of us learn to live our lives somewhere between these two extremes of deprivation and indulgence. As we grow up we are caught up in a pattern of looking first and foremost to self. The ego comes to reign supreme. This is a problem! This is a disease! The rich young ruler needed deliverance, and you and I need deliverance! This is what Jesus brought us, if only we can be caught up in its possibilities.

Prayer Can Pry

I have found release expressed in certain prayers of Michel Quoist, a Roman Catholic Priest. He has written some of the finest prayers that I have read recently; prayers that help me pry loose the roots of my own egotism.

In his book, *Prayers*, Fr. Quoist offers some deep insight into the dilemma that traps modern men. Egotism victimizes and shrivels our capacity to love. We are finally condemned to being able to love only ourselves.

Though often unclear to the victim, the result is the most painful form of personal suffering. Loneliness and alienation linger as personal tormentors. Inwardly, the egotist is crying for someone to come as light and hope to bring release to himself. The Christian is this very means back to joy.

What can a Christian bring that will unlock and break the chains of self? Quoist suggests a simple little prayer will be sufficient. If sincerity and real personal insight stand behind the words, this prayer will be enough. Simply pray, "Lord, deliver me from myself." This will be the first step to wholeness.

"Lord, deliver me from myself."[2]

We too can say such a prayer every night when we come home to escape from ourselves and from other men, and to draw near to God. People have this need when caught in themselves. Vision is lost until someone enters into the mire to redirect and give new possibility.

Out of this the victim may begin to pray, "Lord, deliver me."

Then something can come forth. This means, first and foremost, that for me to escape my problem I must face up to the fact that this is the way life is. I must experience a personal dissatisfaction with my life and must decide to do something about it. I must fully intend to face up to my present existence. Only then will I recognize that I am caught by this cancer, and that whatever it takes I will encounter it and deal with it. That "whatever" will be allowed to work!

This "whatever" may not be at all what we expect. Sometimes it is very painful, an opportunity encased in hardship. Actually it may be happening to us right now. We may feel that this experience is an injustice and an imposition. We may regard it as an undeserved wrong. Yet this trial may do just fine as a "whatever" to force us to see the truth about our motives and our wants. If a life experience moves us to pray sincerely, "Lord, deliver me from myself," it is God's opportunity.

I am convinced that as God does His chastening and correcting work in us, many of us have to go over the same ground again and again because we just don't pay attention the first time around. Have you ever watched football players running through tires? They do it until they've got the fundamentals right. In the military, trainees have to repeat certain exercises until they are completely strengthened. Unfortunately some of us have to be taught by God many times before we get the lesson right! We just don't seem to get it until we have first really become dissatisfied.

Someone may need to enter our lives and bring us that quality that Quoist called "light and joy." Perhaps we have seen this promise embodied in someone else's life. You may have to seek out such a person. They are really all around if you know where to look. The best place to look is usually in a church. Perhaps some famous religious leader might come to mind. Sam Shoemaker and Frank Laubach provided such illumination for me.

But, let me suggest that you don't look only to the famous. Seek out some simple, "everybody" type of person who sits rather obscurely in a pew and looks like you! First find out about his spiritual discoveries, and then he can probably tell you about the rest of the way quite easily.

A house painter named Irwin Tinker was the big turning point in my life. He and his little wife were very "everybody" people filled with the Spirit of Christ. What I saw in their unselfish ministry to collegiates spoke volumes of theology. Their simple sharing of the unselfish life was my "light and joy."

Satisfied? You've Missed!

There is absolutely no hope for the satisfied man. If you have been reading this thinking it really applies to someone else, you've missed it. I'm sorry, but you may say, "This is me! This is where I am! This is the problem that haunts my existence! I'm deeply dissatisfied with my life and I'm going to do something about it." Until you move in that direction, you are stuck on dead center. And you will have a dead center inside you!

Once I am dissatisfied with myself, the first thing I must learn to do is to quit projecting guilt to other people, and to begin taking responsibility for my own life. A characteristic of the self-preoccupied person is that his own problem is always somebody else's fault.

Martha said, "It's Mary." The rich young ruler said, "It's my money." The wife says, "It's my husband." The husband says, "It's my wife." The kids say, "It's my parents." The parents say, "It's those kids." It's always somebody else's fault! Until we decide to take responsibility for every condition and every situation in which we are involved, we will continue to go around and around in that same vicious and self-centered circle.

Jesus said to the rich young ruler, "Get with it! Stand up! Do it! Sell everything!" I'm not sure He was talking about money in the usual sense. I believe that Jesus was seeing money as a symbol of the perimeters of the ruler's life that kept others out and kept himself in. Jesus was saying, "You've got to break the barriers."

Whatever it is, from now on I have to stand up and say, "In Christ's name, I'm going to be responsible. I will exercise that responsibility totally. I recognize the problem. I accept responsibility for my life. In the midst of accepting responsibility for the things I have done, I'm going to venture forth and break new relationships open and break away from my dead center. With God's help I'm going to reach out for others. I will do what must be done to broaden my emotional perimeters."

It is a psychological truism that to deal with the problem of egotism you must learn to love someone else in the same degree as you love yourself. Of course this is very hard, and sometimes it begins as pure drudgery. But as emotions open, a crack widens and something starts to open in our lives. We may have to force ourselves into these relationships.

The woman caught in chronic boredom came to see that there was no cure for her problem except to become involved with and concerned for somebody else to a significant degree. Shortly after our talk, a girl came through town who had been left by her husband. She was very young and now utterly destitute. This woman became involved with her and took the young lady's problems upon herself. These were hard, difficult problems, yet she helped clothe her, helped provide for her, and helped her find educational opportunities. It was at this point that the woman's chronic, self-centered boredom began to precipitate and die.

Dicken's immortal story of Ebenezer Scrooge, in *Christmas Carol*, is the tale of another poor rich man. We love this tale of Christmas because we sense that it is every man's story. We all must struggle with our own ghosts to avoid becoming locked to our past. Only in a radical conversion to other-centeredness can we be free. Real happiness is the by-product of meaningful living that springs from sharing life with other people.

Three Crucial Concepts

The Christian faith is really built around three word concepts. Have you ever heard the Greek word *kerygma*? This summarizes the complete proclamation of Christ. We may hear it in various forms, but at its heart it is the good news. There is hope for our condition, and this hope is found in Jesus Christ.

In the New Testament the kerygma is tied to another word. *Koinonia* is the community of those who have experienced new hope in Jesus Christ right now. Koinonia means fellowship. Once you discover that Jesus frees you from self-imprisonment, you will be pulled into a new group of people who share life together. Actually, this is what the church is really all about.

There is a third word called the *diakonia*. It means service. After you have found what an amazing thing it is to share in koinonia, you just have to take it out into the world. So the Christian message takes you from *hearing that you can be free* to a new role of *being a world changer*. That's quite a trip! The Christian life is not intended to be only "accepting the message." It is *entering into a fellowship* where we lose ourselves in others and start serving.

We could call our era the age of the rich young rulers. It is a time of young men who have affluence and ease but who cannot find happiness. Any modern novel, any modern movie, shares this same scene of people who have everything material but are floating in a great, great emptiness.

What's the answer? We need to put in some moral overtime in examining how we feel about other people. We must invest ourselves on behalf of others. As we do, we will be surprised to hear Jesus saying, "That's it! That's how you sell it all, and, in selling it all, that's where you find life!"

When Jesus speaks to us like this, it is always in a particular context. You must understand this clearly in order to get the message straight. I'm not suggesting that you try to change yourself. Does that sound paradoxical? It is. "Breaking our shell" is something we do ourselves, but the message of Jesus Christ is that "selling all" is not something we do by ourselves. To have my center really changed is a matter of knowing the dynamic power of the Holy Spirit moving in and through my life. Apart from this, my struggling can become wasted effort.

We must both make the necessary effort to do our part and to open our lives to the Holy Spirit's power. That's where it all begins to happen. For some of us it's opening those encrusted doors that we have intentionally fastened shut. It is asking the Holy Spirit to break open what we can't budge and to sensitize our lives. He must work down within the wellsprings of our life, opening us up to others. That can be painful, but it is so, so healing.

It is not enough for me to tell you and for you to tell me this is true. We must pray with every intention, "Father, make me more sensitive, make me more open."

Further, I have discovered that for renewal to take powerful shape, it's also a matter of meditation.

Meditation is really a very old Christian experience which simply means prayerfully thinking with God. I pray and I think and I do these things together. It is like chewing, like carefully masticating food. Mentally, spiritually I chew up this truth of God. I struggle in prayer, "Father, help me think through this need." I think about it from my end, then I pray about it from God's end. Out of that matrix of the Holy Spirit and me, God begins to make things clear, to make things different, and I am changed.

Action Is Your Answer

Here's how God is remolding me. When I pray about my egotism, almost always I learn certain actions I must take. There is nothing mystical about this; if you take the time, it will happen to you too. Most often God will tell you something you didn't want to hear, and it may well be something you didn't expect. He may ask you to give or to make restitution. He may ask you to open yourself, open your home, or open your pocket. You'll find yourself saying, "Heavens, how did I get into this?" But as you see direction, get up and do it! In doing what God directs, healing will begin to pour into your life. You will find yourself moving from selfishness to otherness. The rich young man went home sorrowful, but you will go home rejoicing.

Healing doesn't come as much while we sit quietly praying as when we follow what God has shown us during prayer. It will be the beginning of the most exciting discoveries of your life.

There are many dimensions to what Jesus taught. "If a man loses his life he'll find it, and the man who keeps his life will lose it." You must be willing to sell all to apprehend to the fullest what God wants to give you.

Remember, when I say that we are sinful persons, I'm not simply saying that we are "bad." We must recognize that it's much deeper than that. We all want to be the center of the world; we all want to make everything revolve around ourselves. But to really find life, we must move to another basis of operation. I promise you that if you draw near to God's healing potential in this way, He will do something so powerful in your life that it will make you into a new person!

This came in a fresh way to me just recently. Very early one morning I received a long-distance phone call from a friend, who told me that a dear friend of his had finally died of cancer. I remember this girl so well. She was one of the first girls in our youth group in Oklahoma City.

Through the years, I watched Cindy slowly move in a most wholesome way, into a very other-centered person in Christ. She went off to college and met a guy who was going to be a minister. Christ moved her and rotated her to more other-centeredness. A year ago she was diagnosed with a very painful, abdominal type of cancer.

One thing that calling in hospitals has taught me is that pain makes people very self-centered. When you hurt, all in the world that matters is that you hurt. But Cynthia struggled with her pain, intending that Christ would be the center, and that others could see the reflection. When someone asked, "How are you doing?" she would never give a direct answer, because she wanted to have you talk about something other than her condition. She didn't often tell anybody how difficult it was.

Her father was a doctor, so he knew how very painful it was to deteriorate in this way. Finally, on Friday morning, in the throes of what he knew was tremendous agony, he had to wake her up.

She said, "Daddy, this is going to be a good day." Then, one by one, she began to give everyone in her family a special message. Her father could not believe that she could endure the whole day. Yet she kept herself alive by focusing on others. Finally, at about five that afternoon, she told her family she loved them and then simply went to sleep.

It was a total witness of how powerfully Christ can turn our self-centeredness into other-centeredness. Jesus said to Cindy, "Sell it all, whatever it takes, that you might find the abundance of life." She did, and it touched every life around her with love. Cindy had every right to expect attention to be focused on her needs and hurts. Instead, she gave out warmth and concern that comforted her comforters. Her life became too abundant to die. Cynthia just went to sleep one afternoon on a bright summer day.

Some Helps to Wholeness

Why not do something about the burden of "yourself" right now? The promise is wholeness. The only enemy is self-centeredness. Again, praying is the starting point. Why not use these words to get started? Then silently listen within to see if you can discern any action you need to take.

Gracious Father, help me to realize the joy that I can know by getting outside my egotism. Help me to have the courage to be dissatisfied, to face the truth, to take the responsibility, and to let you make things different. As I start this new journey, just now I want to open myself to the fullness of your Holy Spirit's love and power. Please move in and through me, making me sensitive. Heal me, that I may become like our Lord, who was always a man for others. In His name, Amen.

For Further Consideration

1. Apply the 10 questions on page 46 to yourself. How do you really stack up?
2. How did you honestly feel when I called you a "sinner"? Did it sound old-fashioned? Did it make you defensive? Did you want to laugh it off? What is the truth of the issue?
3. Are you satisfied with your life? If you're not, where are your real dissatisfactions?
4. What could really happen if you began to pray, "Lord, deliver me from myself"? Where might God start to work on you?
5. Fantasize a bit. What practical things might happen if you decided to really "lose" your life?

Footnotes

1. Charles Kingsley, *All Saints' Day* (New York: Scribner, Armstrong and Co., 1878).
2. Michel Quoist, *Prayers* (New York: Sheed and Ward, 1963), p. 111.

4
ESCAPISM
CHECKING OUT

She was a deeply troubled young woman. She talked about her problems with a tenseness and urgency that betrayed inner anguish and pain. These were very real and difficult issues. In talking about her problems, we shared all the ramifications and the scope of what was wrong, what had to happen, the alternatives and the possibilities. Then I asked what she was going to do.

Her response was, "I think I'm going to run. I think I'm going to just disappear. I just want to escape. I want to get away from it all and fly into the night."

These very words could have been repeated verbatim five or six times in numerous counseling sessions I had had in the immediately preceding weeks. When life becomes overwhelming, retreat is a most familiar response. When the alternatives seem so overwhelming, we all have the tendency to look at the difficulties and respond, "I want to run. I want to disappear." Christian or non-Christian, one of the most natural reactions to the apprehensive things of life is fast retreat.

Retreat seems natural, but it leads nowhere. Let's look at how these empty responses rob us of the joy and spirituality that ought to be ours. Escapism is the problem. It is the pattern of running away from problems as a way of resolving them. It can become a pattern of life.

Let's see if we can put you into the picture. Is this response to life uncommon with you? It's certainly common with me. When caught in a tough dilemma, I naturally find myself checking where the back doors are located. On many an occasion I would rather have "checked out" than dealt with the problem.

To put it squarely before you, let me assume the role of a playwright. Drama is like a mirror; in the actors we see our own reflection and find ourselves revealed in their lives. It is our virtues and vices that they depict.

I want to hold up a mirror to show both virtue and vice and to reflect back to you where you are. I'd like you to think I'm just saying, "Look; what do you see?" Is it possible that I'm talking to you? It is a very natural thing to want to run. I understand this, but I must insist that it is a defeating path to an unproductive way of life.

Your Reflection?

Let me hold up for you a bit of literature that is one of these mirrors. Henrik Ibsen, the great Norwegian writer, portrayed life very poignantly. In one of his plays the central character was named Peer Gynt. Young Peer goes out into the forest and by accident sees another young man cutting off his finger with a knife. As Peer sees this, he knows immediately what is happening: The other youth is maiming himself so he cannot be drafted into the military.

Peer says to himself, "Aha! This is a profitable way

to face life! Always keep all your options open. Never get yourself boxed in. Never get yourself committed. Always keep yourself in a position of being able to retreat."

Later Peer says to some of his disciples, "The essence of the art of daring, of bravery in action, is this: to stand with choice-free foot amidst the treacheries of life, to know for sure that other days remain beyond the battle, to know ever in the rear a bridge stands open to bear me over."[1]

This is Peer's philosophy of life: Always be ready to escape; never be committed to the finish; always be tentative in all your plans.

Doesn't that sound contemporary? Peer Gynt could be living in our same block. His escapism has become a style of life that all varieties of people have learned to live out! Always be ready for retreat!

As the story unfolds, Ibsen leads his hero to discover the truth. Peer's behavior is really cowardly and ultimately destructive; it is empty and hollow. Though it escapes the dilemma at hand, it doesn't finally solve any problems. It is a completely defeating way to live.

What do you see in this mirror? I see that escapism as a way of approaching life's problems is always hopeless, destructive, and frustrating! We must have a better alternative. If we do not, we find ourselves cutting off noses to avoid dealing with faces, removing fingers to spare hands, and slicing toes to preserve feet. In the end we are crippled, and the problems still remain. No one wants to think of himself as being a coward, but here are the issues. By the way, what did you see in that mirror I held up?

Take a Second Look!

For a better solution let's pick up where we left off in

the last chapter. Much of what I am writing in this book is really an exposition of Jesus' words, "He who finds his life will lose it, and he who loses his life for my sake will find it" (Matt. 10:39, *RSV*). We need to decipher this emotionally as well as doctrinally.

When we talk about these verses of Scripture we usually think of them in the context of conversion or as a way of encountering the life of Jesus Christ in a redeeming way. Let me suggest that this is not only a theological principle, but that it also has psychological implications. The man who is willing to lose his life in Christ, who is not afraid to let everything go for the Master, is the man who finds true life. The man who is always trying to keep life secure, to save it and hold it for another day, is the man who ultimately loses it.

From the psychological point of view, the lesson we must learn is to hit life head-on for Christ's sake. It is in this forward thrust, underwritten by the power of the life of Christ in us, that we will solve our problems and find the ability to live life successfully! Straightforward encounter will give us a new dynamic and a new sense of fulfillment, regardless of the outcome of the problem at hand.

To fulfill Christ's promise in our lives will take some reflection. First, we will have to realize that it is neither natural nor comfortable to be willing to lay down our lives and to live with honesty. We must recognize that escapism is a very natural tendency; let's recognize this within ourselves. All of us must discover that escapism is a normal reflex. For example, a child who touches a hot stove will quickly learn to draw back his hand! As we grow older we learn that the quickest, easiest way out of painful situations is to retreat. Yes, escaping is natural!

But take a second look at the results.

Jonah, Jeremiah, and You

Through all of Scripture we find escapism portrayed honestly and realistically wherever it occurs. The Bible never conceals anything; it states with candor the way things really are.

Remember Elijah? Here was a courageous prophet! He was a great prophet who was fearless in his battle with evil. Again and again, armed only with the Word of the Lord, he sallied forth to the conflict. Yet the years of toil took their toll. Wearied with the strife, and fearful for his life, Elijah reached his own point of retreat. He found himself wanting out, wanting to escape the confrontation with Jezebel and avoid the awesome emotional strain (see 1 Kings 19).

What other Old Testament character reminds you of retreat? I always think of Jonah. The Lord said to him, "Go tell this people a hard thing." Every minister eventually gets the hard thing to say, and he identifies with Jonah.

The Lord said, "Go to Nineveh and tell them they must repent." You know the story. Jonah checked out and ran. His story reminds us that whenever you try to run, there is always an accounting that follows. I cannot easily be critical of Jonah, for I realize that any minister who stands before his people, looks them right in the eye, and tells them in scathing terms of their wrong, knows how very natural it is to want to run!

The psalmist expresses how escape feels. He could have written about our desire to retreat a hundred times: "The terrors of death have fallen upon me. Fear and trembling come upon me, and horror overwhelms me. And I say, 'O that I had wings like a dove! I would fly away and be at rest' " (Ps. 55:4-6, *RSV*). David would like to run, to hide in the shelter! He knows what it's like to be scared to death!

Jeremiah found the same feeling. Jeremiah was perhaps one of the greatest preachers who ever lived, preaching with fury again and again. Finally he came to the place where he thought he could contend with the people no longer! He too might have cried, "If I could hide in the wilderness!"

However, we remember psalmist and prophet alike—not because of their tendency to do what they felt like doing, but because in the face of checking out—did the opposite! They did the diametrically opposed thing. Rather than retreating, they hit life head-on! The psalmist in these same verses gives us the clue.

After he gets in touch with his deepest emotions, David says, "This is the truth—He will deliver my soul in safety from the battle that I wage." What David learned was that the power of God is not intended to keep us from battle, but to empower us right in the midst of the struggle—to take us through it all.

If I'm going to receive all that God is going to give me for my life, I don't ask Him to take me on an evasive route. He doesn't lead me under or around the problems, but His power takes me right through them.

I have to resist my natural tendency and dare to live through my problems by and with the power of God. Jeremiah wanted to retreat, but he didn't. He came back and hit the conflicts again and again until he finally died with those people. What a powerful fulfillment! He knew that the power of God would take him through, and it did!

Martin Luther is a graphic example of going *through* life rather than around it. After the Reformation began, Luther was under attack and his life was threatened. If he fell into enemy hands he would be killed very quickly. For his safety, Luther's friends decided to place him in a high fortress overlooking the Rhine River.

There no one could attack. But in the security of the castle, Luther began to reflect on his life. With everything secure around him, he began to despair. He wrote a letter to Philipp Melanchthon with the words, "Philipp, everything is lost, everything is lost! There is no hope!"

Then Luther left the castle. He came out of the secure place where everything was safe and intact. Going right back into life without any security or certainty, and knowing that his life would be in danger, he wrote, "A mighty fortress is our God, a bulwark never failing." It was *in the battle* that Luther discovered the power of God!

Let's go through life, not *around* it!

Any Escape Artists in Your Family?

Let's look at another dimension of the problem. Escapism is a modern way of life! Society is immersed in this method of problem-avoidance. Because escapism has permeated our daily life, its pervasive effects are heightened; our commitments, our values, and ultimately our mission in life is subtly eroded and corroded with cowardice.

Tell me, is this not today's world? Perhaps Peer Gynt lives in your block, in your house! Think for a few minutes—how do realtors advertise a new housing development? Every time we turn on the radio we hear, "It's a place to escape from it all!" "Come to Escape Country!"

Retreat has become the hallmark of the suburbs; it is a hallmark of our way of life. We retreat to where we live; we draw our curtains around ourselves and wish to push all others out.

Recently I was talking with someone about life in such a suburb, where we don't want to know anybody and instead want to keep everything secure. We observed how this atmosphere cripples our thinking.

History and psychology both warn us what happens when there is an increase in comfort and a decrease in discipline; the result is always a softening of character. Anytime there is a growth of affluence and a corresponding lessening of demand, you can bet that this combination will not produce strong, tenacious, tough people.

This phenomenon has a great deal to say about how you and I raise our children. It has a lot to say about what we put into our children, and with what we confront them. What a danger it is to have their thinking infected! Without realizing it, we raise them to be people whose style of life is avoidance rather than engagement. There is escapism in our families!

Burt Lancaster, being interviewed on one of TV's talk shows, told how he got into the movies. He shared an amazing story of how he began with the circus.

At an audition he was asked to perform on the parallel bars, so he leaped on the bars and began his routine. Because he was nervous, his timing was off, and he spun over the bar, falling flat on his face some 10 feet below. He was so humiliated that he immediately leaped back on the bar. As he spun again at the same point, he flipped off and smashed to the ground once more!

Burt's tights were torn, he was cut and bleeding, and he was fiercely upset! He leaped back again, but the third time was even worse, for this time he fell on his back. The agent came over, picked him up, and said, "Son, if you won't do that again, you've got the job!"

As I listened and watched, I thought, "That's the key to fantastic charisma! That's what makes him such a powerful figure! " Burt Lancaster has that built-in sense that nothing will defeat him. "If it kills me, I'll do it again until I've conquered it."

That's power! We've got to put that in our kids and in ourselves! It is for Christ's sake that we need to learn to hit life head-on!

Bamboozled, Boozed, and Bored!

We just do not meet life very well at all. The statistics demonstrate this very clearly. Hearing some of the facts on the radio, I wrote the statistics down because I could not believe they were true—that we have had to meet life that artificially! Last year in the United States over *300 million* prescriptions were written for tranquilizers! That represents something over *50 billion* tablets! Think about it! Three hundred million prescriptions to artificially deal with life because we can't face it head-on!

In the United States today are nearly 7 million alcoholics and over 12 million dependent drinkers![2] A large chunk of that problem has occurred because people have not learned to adjust to life. What makes Alcoholics Anonymous so powerful? Through their 12-step program, people are taught how to face reality and to engage themselves in life again. They learn how to face life honestly rather than by retreating.

Since we are on the subject, I want to add something else. Statistics tell me that every time I look at an audience, it contains a number of people who have a drinking problem. In the church too? Sure, we hide it best in a church! Unfortunately, we feel that alcoholism refers only to the guy in the gutter, the fellow who is really down and out. The truth is that this is only the last stage of alcoholism.

Actually, alcoholism has three rather distinct phases: early, middle, and late. If we learn to solve problems and take care of tensions by regularly and consistently consuming alcohol, we qualify for the first stage. If this definition offends you, then you really do qualify for the first stage.

Does this bother you? Then I want you to try something: Try going 30 days without touching a drop of alcohol. Going a month without alcohol won't prove that you *don't* have a problem with alcohol, but if you can't do it, this is a sure sign that you *do* have a problem! In fact, your problem could be the beginning of very serious trouble.

Alcoholism is a disease that goes from this stage to the middle stage, and then continues on until they sweep you off the stage! Don't kid yourself—if you have to respond to life by escape through alcohol, it will finally eat you alive!

Let me add one more example of our society's current preoccupation with retreat. Recently I ran across a fascinating article that described the new man of the 1970's. The writer was contrasting the 70's man with the man of the 50's and 60's in American life. Today we have a new type of man called "psychological man." This is the man whose primary concern is the enjoyment of his environment. This new man will avoid unprofitable and unpleasurable commitments. If there is too much demand on him or too much involvement, he simply withdraws. He has become the ultimate product of a consumer society. He is neither a great villain nor a great hero; he is simply a floater. Does that sound like a lot of people in your hometown? This man in the new society will not commit himself to anything that takes too much time or commitment. He cannot be depended on to be responsible.[3]

Here is the bigger jolt! The new man of the 70's carries a surprise hidden behind his nonchalance. The ultimate end of his noncommittal style is despair. Unhappiness shrouds his life; satisfaction dissolves like county-fair cotton candy; existential dread sours the life of ease; the bottom line totals emptiness.

Surprising? It shouldn't be. Earlier in this century, T.S. Eliot warned of the road ahead. His poem "The Hollow Men," prophesied that straw-stuffed heads would dissolve from the scene in silent whispers of despair. For the shallow, "the world ends not with a bang but a whimper." The ultimate end of escapism is a whine.

Face up to the facts! Not only is escapism an unsuccessful way of life, it is the road to emptiness. The floaters drift on to oblivion.

Here Are Two Answers!

Since avoidance and evasion are so unacceptable, what must I do with life so that it will not reduce me to a straw man? There are several things I need to know.

The first is that most of us retreat because we have not found an adequate foundation on which to stand. Our retreat is symbolic of our fearfulness about the adequacy of our life's base.

This is true for Christians too. You and I may be very much within the church, and we may very strongly affirm Jesus Christ as Lord, but we still may not have found that Jesus Christ is the ultimately secure foundation on which our lives can stand.

Many of us live a long time without discovering that Jesus is final security. The first thing that allows me to stand up against "the way it is" is the personal realization that deep within my being my God is able.

Here's a surprise! The second answer is the opposite of what we would expect. The power of God is not given to help us escape trouble; God's divine encouragement and enablement is found as it *takes us through problems.* God's power is not for the armchair quarterback;

69

it is the man *in the midst of the fight* who finds God's power adequate for his life's problems. When you are in the fight, you are closest to His help!

Here is a crucial ingredient in understanding life as a Christian. I've got a little sign on my wall, "Things which hurt instruct! The things that are painful teach!"

When I am in the midst of my struggles, and everything in me says "run," I need to know that here is God's golden opportunity to teach me something that can be taught in no other way. If it hurts, I come to see that pain is the way in which the broken, closed doors of my life are repaired and pulled open. It is in the hard, hurtful things that I am made vulnerable, and that something new can be born.

We live with the feeling that we have a right to be happy all the time. We think everything should be great. Why should anything bad happen to you and me? The truth is that nobody has such a right.

God in His graciousness does not withhold life as it really is. If He did, it would make us insipid. That's where straw men—hollow men—come from, and why they are empty. They are the people who have never lived life in its depth.

It is in the depths and the hardness that God teaches us what we must know. I have learned this only by going head-on into the midst of living.

There is a little poem that I go back and read when I am just about at the end of my rope. It goes like this:

> Did you tackle that trouble
>   that came your way
> With a resolute heart and cheerful?
> Or hide your face from the light of day,
> With a craven soul and fearful?
> Oh, troubles a ton and troubles an ounce,
> And trouble is what you make it.

It isn't the fact that you hurt that counts,
But how did you take it?
You're beaten to the earth?
Well, what's that?
Come up with a smiling face.
It's nothing against you to fall down flat,
But to lie there, that's disgrace.
The harder you're thrown,
  the higher you bounce;
Be proud of your blackened eye.
It isn't the fact that you're licked
  that counts,
It's how did you fight and why?
And though you be done to the death,
What then?
You've battled the best that you could.
If you played your part in the world of men,
Why, the Critic will call it good.
Death comes with a crawl or death comes
  with a pounce,
And whether he's slow or spry,
It isn't the fact that you're dead that counts,
It's only how did you die?[4]

From Cemetery to Success

What did Jesus say? "He who loses his life will find
it." The escapist reverses this formula, for he is afraid to
let go. Dying is his total fear; he wants to hold on to
everything! Jesus came to say, "No! It is letting go.
Once you have faced this, you can really live."

Many of us are defeated Christians because we have
never died to ourselves. We are so tied to our pettiness
and vested interests that we cannot see beyond the
limits of our navels. Our horizon lines start and end with
the tip of our nose. Our inordinate desire for security

71

robs us of the heroic dimension that makes us whole persons.

Our Christian faith always has two parts—*my* death and Christ's life. Often it is only as I am utterly crushed that I can know I am not sufficient. It is then I find His life to be completely adequate. When I come to the end of my own life, then I find the totality of *His* life.

Where is the power? Where is the force? Where is the promise? It is always one step beyond my last resort. When I have come to my last alternative, then I stand on the edge of finding all of Christ's promise. It is only as I die to myself that I really live to Him.

This is exactly what Paul meant when he wrote to the Galatian church, "I have been crucified with Christ; it is no longer I who live, but Christ who lives in me" (Gal. 2:20, *RSV*).

And to the Corinthian church, in his second letter, he wrote, "At that time we were completely overwhelmed; the burden was more than we could bear; in fact we told ourselves that this was the end. Yet we believe now that we had this experience of coming to the end of our tether that we might learn to trust, not in ourselves, but in God who can raise the dead" (2 Cor. 1:8,9, *Phillips*).

Resurrection power works best in cemeteries. Would I dare to move to a cemetery? Just how much of me was I willing to bury on behalf of Jesus Christ? Dare I take my dreams, hopes, and ambitions to be sacrificed for His sake? Christ's promise is that this cemetery holds the key to real success. Jesus tells me that only as I have faced death to these areas can I really live! Such a critical self-examination may be part of a cemetery experience as far as your ego is concerned, but it's a critically important part of the path to personal spiritual power.

There's a little song that has helped me find this power. In the early 60's you would have had to live in the South and Southwest to understand this fully. Many of us were involved in the civil rights struggle. There were thousands of people living in humiliation and degradation, and times were bad. The church set out to see if we could change that. Meetings were held in those little black churches that were so poor and so decrepit. In the midst of this, people would say, "It can't be done. They'll never let us ride in the front of those buses." People needed a battle song to keep their spirits up and to allow them to see beyond the complexities at hand.

Then things began to unfold. Part of what made the action believable was the song that became the hallmark of the civil rights movement. "We shall overcome, we shall overcome someday." We would sing that again and again, and people who had learned always to retreat would suddenly stand up and say, "In my heart I know that we shall overcome. The Lord will protect, the Lord will give peace." Everybody locked arms and went forward. And we overcame!

When you're "up agin it" and you don't believe there is any hope, try humming, "We shall overcome." "We" means you and Jesus Christ. You and Christ will overcome. Whatever you are confronted with, it doesn't matter! You might even know that you may lose—or even die. "You shall overcome." Christ's power will not let you fall to despair or become a hollow man. It will make you a strong person of integrity, rooted and grounded in Him.

Some Helps to Wholeness

So now's the time to quit running! You can stop "checking out" on the things that really matter. Remember, you're not in this by yourself. The personal presence of Jesus Christ will supply what you lack. Why not pause and make this an accomplished fact? If you're not sure of the right words, start with the following prayer.

Gracious heavenly Father, give me the faith that overcomes. Give me fight in the midst of the battle. When I would retreat, I know that this is the very point at which you will lead me beyond my personal capacity. I want to live on that level. Coming to the end of my rope and my sufficiency is the key to your complete supply. Envelop my life in the complete adequacy of all things being possible in Jesus Christ. Amen.

For Further Consideration

1. Read through Psalm 55. Can you identify with this? How and why?
2. Explore and write down some of the things that make you want to run.
3. Prayerfully consider how God could actually use each one of these things to further develop your abilities and strengthen your life.
4. How would you measure yourself against the description of a modern psychological man?
5. What does it mean for you personally when we say, "The things that hurt, instruct!"? Have you found this to be true?

Footnotes

1. Henrik Ibsen, *Peer Gynt* (Garden City, N.Y., Anchor Books, Doubleday and Co., 1963).
2. *Alcohol, Who Is Allergic?* (Seattle, WN., Enzomedic Laboratories, Inc., 123 S.W. 157th Street).
3. Robert Berne, *Wandering in the Wilderness* (Philadelphia: Fortress Press, 1972), pp. 24-42.
4. Edmund Vance Cooke, "How Did You Die," in *Masterpieces of Religious Verse*, ed. James Dalton Morrison (New York: Harper and Broghers, 1948).

5
CHANGE
THE HOODED BANDIT

There is a hooded bandit who steals into our best moments and snatches away the joy of all that is familiar. Ruthlessly he drains away the nectar of our children's youth, and in a swirl of dust they have grown, stolen from our homes by this relentless villain. The security of "the way it was" dissolves at this touch, and we are left with the disconcerting emptiness of the new and different. Streets, houses, friends—even our faces and bodies—are all prey to his relentless attack.

This bandit's name is Change. His abode is universal; he is the one who stirs up the churning place as this is the disorienting disorganizer. You cannot escape his coming and going.

We don't like this bandit called Change. Something in us is bothered by the fact that we can never quite preserve things as we want them. The best experiences, the best moments, the really inspiring times are gone so quickly.

We secretly think, "I want to keep my kids this age forever; I want to somehow hold them right here; I don't want them to keep going on."

Or we don't want our parents to get older. We don't want our home or a favorite building to change; we don't want our particular way of life to stop. We know just how Peter felt. You and I want to take "now" and nail it down tight. I want to keep this time forever!

Part of every pastor's experience in ministering to people is to struggle together with them in facing change. The frightening uncertainty of life has often arisen as I sat down with people to talk about the problems of death, marriage, or business. Together we lament what change is doing to us. We don't like it; we want to stop it.

For many of us it is a real emotional problem to know how we can live our lives in the midst of the increased flow of events today. Particularly for us who live in this last half of the twentieth century, with all its accelerated communication and other changes coming at such an increasing rate, all the pressures of change come down on us in a particularly heavy way. It all gets out of hand.

Why My Father Resisted Change
Let me share a couple of incidents in my own life. I was always irritated by how my father regarded change. When I was young I felt very unsympathetic with his reluctance to accept the changing scene, but in recent years I have begun to discover the source of his reservations. This discovery has helped me see why we resist change, and that much of our reluctance is based on valid reasons.

76

My grandmother came to Oklahoma in a covered wagon. A neighboring tribe of Indians tried to trade blankets and horses for my father when he was a baby! In this plains area of western Oklahoma he went to school and grew to manhood. In the developing community of Clinton, my grandfather built most of the houses in their end of town.

This is still my father's neighborhood. Most of his life has been lived within about 30 miles of the sod house where my grandmother and grandfather pioneered. There is something within him that resists any kind of change to this scenery!

As the flow of events has come so fast in the last few years, I began to realize what terrific pressures this placed on my father's world. It is true that a rut can be only slightly more shallow than a grave, yet in his world "sameness" offers marvelous stability and very reassuring predictability; it gives life a seeming security. I've come to respect how good it can feel when everyday life is clear, defined, and predictable.

But for most of us our circumstances do not remain stable; unless we can accept the inevitable changes comfortably, they will become a real emotional problem for us. Things really do change: Sod houses wash away, little boys grow whiskers, little girls start wearing make-up, black hair begins to be corrupted by the betraying strands of gray, and someday we must stand beside the crypt of the dearest one in our world. *Things really do change.*

I observed the power of transitions in a child-care center we operated in our Oklahoma City church. We provided care for the children of divorced mothers who needed help while they worked.

A beautiful little baby came to us at six months of age. Penny developed in that 10-by-10-foot crib room. At age two it was time for her to go out of that very comfortable little room where she had lived most of her life. Now she had the opportunity to go across the hall to a new big room where the toddlers played. I had never thought of it as being large. But that room was actually about three times the size of the first one.

One morning we said, "Penny, we have a surprise." We took her across the hall and introduced her to this exciting big room. For one whole month she walked around its edges holding onto the walls! She would not let go of the wall to venture out to the center. It was too fearful. Suddenly her world had become too big for this small person to comprehend; change was too frightening.

Sound familiar? Sure, it happens to many of us these days. The walls seem to get larger and farther apart. The familiar vanishes. So how do we handle this? How do we experience overwhelming change and yet be competent for what life is asking of us?

Jesus, Peter, and Change

I find a clue in the story of Peter and the Transfiguration. Peter, James, and John were taken by Jesus high up on a hillside where they were quite alone. There Christ's whole appearance changed before their eyes—He shone like the sun. His clothes were white like light, and Moses and Elijah began talking to Him.

"Lord," exclaimed Peter, "it's wonderful for us to be here. If you like, I could put up three shelters, one for you, one for Moses, and one for Elijah."

But while Peter was talking, a bright light overshadowed them and a voice came out of the cloud saying, "This is my dearly beloved Son, in whom I am well pleased; listen to Him." When they heard the voice, the disciples fell on their faces, overcome with fear, and

78

Jesus came to them and said, "Get up, don't be afraid." As they raised their eyes there was no one to be seen but Jesus Himself. (See Matt. 17:1-8.)

This is an incredible story, and we could talk about its many amazing ramifications. For one thing, it culminated many Old Testament understandings of prophecy and history. What a powerful confirmation it demonstrated!

But I want to pick up the way in which Peter reacted to this event. What he wanted to do as he beheld this sight of immense proportion was a very human thing. Here in light and sound was an awesome event; who could understand what was before them? Peter's reaction in the midst of this wonderful encounter was, "Let's build three buildings so that we can have this moment so this experience will never cease to be! This wonderful moment can be held forever; we won't let anything change." But a voice came out of the clouds, proclaiming the magnificence of Jesus. As the disciples looked up, only Jesus was left. Already in that very moment everything had changed!

I think Peter's response to the Transfiguration was utterly typical of how all of us feel about life. In a burst of light his image of Jesus was changed. Peter's typical reaction can lead us to a new source of assurance.

Peter was being shown that the only constant in a changing world is the person of Jesus Christ. As awesome as that holy moment of worship was, in a few minutes it was over. All that was left was the Lord Jesus Christ.

There is a parable here so large that I find it hard to wrap my mind around it. In fact, I can only proclaim it. Only by living with this truth can I hope to fathom its depth. It is a simple fact that everything else in this universe is going to change and disappear. The only tangible constant in all of creation is the person of Jesus Christ. Everything else is going to deteriorate, erode, and disappear. In the end, all that will stand is the person of Jesus Christ, our Lord. That is a mind-boggler!

Here is the answer to one of the age-old quests of man that has always intrigued thinking and feeling people. It was the very problem that started Plato thinking and caused him to develop his world-shaping philosophy.

He was bothered by the fact that nothing stayed the same. Looking in a mirror, he beheld a paradox. Yesterday I looked one way; today I look this way; tomorrow I will look worse! And I don't like the deterioration!

Plato looked around him at all the magnificent buildings and architecture. They kept falling apart. He reasoned that somewhere there had to be something that would stay when the rest was gone. The goal of his whole philosophy was to find out what was real and tangible in an intangible world that would not stick together.

What he could not know is that the only answer is Jesus Christ. Everything you see, everything you hold, everything you can calculate is going to go. Only Jesus Christ will remain. One of the very few persons I have known who could conceptually grasp this was a Sioux Indian missionary to his fellow Indians. Growing up in South Dakota, he intuitively saw this because of the world view held by the Sioux Indians.

From time immemorial, many Indians believe, the world was only plains, animals, game, and the quiet life. It remained this way until white men came. But even though white men are here now and will remain here for some time to come, they too will pass in the end. When they do, life will return to the prairies, the animals, and the quiet life. They believe that everything else is going to vanish.

This is part of what it is to be one of the Indians. In the midst of this environment, this particular Indian discovered that there is one other ingredient that will abide—Jesus Christ! This truth is in his bones.

In the midst of this changing world in which we live, the first thing we can nail down is at least this one fact: If we are going to be able to cope with life and stand against change in the presence of death and disaster, bad times and good times, changing friends and moving across the country, we must see Christ as constant. We can ultimately and finally depend upon one source: Jesus Christ. Everything starts from here.

As we age and live with this truth, at times there will be a melancholy acceptance of the seasons of life. Yet when the winter blizzard comes and the summer electrical storm falls, there will be bedrock undergirding our very foundations. Jesus Christ will stand after the clouds have passed! My security is that He has promised that I will stand with Him.

Change Can Work for You!

The next thing I must do with any new insight is to make it become a constant in my emotional life. After the light and the glory of the mountaintop had vanished, the voice of God reminded the disciples, "This is my beloved Son; hear Him." That's exactly what I have to do in the realm where I live emotionally. I must apply this experience of Peter, James, and John to my own feelings of fear, anxiety, and dread.

For this to happen I must first accept the inevitability of change. It sounds simple, but from counseling with many people I know it isn't. We try to stand against change, but we are like a small pebble in a tidal wave. We think we can perhaps keep our kids or our parents from getting older. At least we're sure we can keep *ourselves* from turning gray! (And with enough Grecian Formula we try to make a stab at it!) But none of it lasts for long.

On the contrary, something healthy begins when I accept reality as it is. One of the dimensions of reality is unavoidable change. I must say to my feelings that this is the way it's going to be! Shoes are just going to wear out. Kids are going to wear out their pants. Some of my most cherished dreams are going to wear out. Some of my favorite self-images are going to wear out. It's going to go on and on and on.

Let's push it a bit further. A second thing that I must come to know emotionally is that this really isn't bad. It's good! Change is one of the vehicles that God uses; change is one of His tools in creation. This is the truth behind the bandit's mask.

Please read this carefully. I am not suggesting that *all* change is good, nor am I saying that all change is God-ordained. That's sloppy thinking and bad theology, and it will get us into a lot of trouble. Certainly there is an evil one in the world, and he causes change also. Certainly God has given us free will, and we can create our own circumstances. Sometimes change comes from evil, sometimes from us, and sometimes we can't tell the difference! All change is not necessarily God-ordained.

However, God has His hand on the throttle of time, and He will use change to His glory. He will at all times use change in a creative way. Hard to believe? Look back over the scope of human history. Look at what change has meant. I believe you will be forced to say that it has ultimately been a moving and creative force. Sure, 1776 was an exciting year. But I don't want to go back and live there. If you think we've got economic problems today, go back and see what it was like to keep alive then. We've come a long way from there.

Remember the classic story of Silas Marner? Silas Marner was caught in the midst of the industrial revolution. His life was forced to change. His is the story of a very narrow man who was enlarged. Human emotion and love changed him. Finally he looked back and found he was freed of the past. This provincial man was surprised to discover that change was creative.

How about Dickens' converted character, Ebenezer Scrooge? He would have to tell you the same thing. Change is redemptive. God uses it as His tool. When I know that and feel it, I can live with things as they are.

It's Not How You Feel

Here's another insight! I get my mind on the *fact* of change, rather than on my *feelings*, as change happens. If I measure everything by how I feel about it, I'll have lots of problems. As a Christian I can't measure everything purely by how I will profit from it. I am called to look at the facts of change and at its movement in a broader perspective than just my own ego. Jesus Christ has saved me from having to measure everything by how I like it.

Change is measured by its effect on the total human community. That's a real problem, because I want to calculate only my personal dividend. If I individually appear to come out short, it's hard to approve of the change for the rest of the race.

You say, "Of course—isn't that a natural tendency?" Right! But Jesus Christ, in calling me to be a man, has at last liberated me from an imprisoning egotism. If it's for the good of the rest, I can praise God for its possibilities.

I learned this principle in western Oklahoma through a local institution found in every small town. It's called the Spit and Whittle Club. In every community there's a corner where some insurance agency has put up benches. The old farmers, cowboys, and Indians sit there in the sun on Saturday afternoons. Everybody has a knife and whittles as he sharpens twigs, discusses life, and spits on the ground. (There's also a special club like this in the state capitol. They usually call it the state legislature!) In Spit and Whittle Clubs you really get at life's ongoing issues and how people feel about them.

As a kid I used to sit and listen for hours to these old guys talk. I learned early that unless the issue profited them first, it never sat well on the Spit and Whittle Club agenda. Later I understood why the meeting always ended with the benediction, "Ain't it awful?" Those who only measure life by the length of their personal interest seem to always end up with bad feelings.

Today I can be free of such self-interest. Jesus Christ gave us the opportunity to love our brother. So in this last half of the twentieth century we must learn to see others' needs as easily as we see our own concerns. Therefore, if I can see that change is ultimately good for my fellowman, I affirm it in spite of myself. The needs of others makes a better yardstick than my own two feet!

This is the same lesson Peter received from the voice of God. Jesus Christ calls me to see everything in the light of eternity. I am to use the perspective of His lordship over the total community. Jesus Christ is the only constant; He is Lord of all. He said, "I am the Alpha and the Omega. After it's all over, my words will endure. My word will judge everything."

Change your focus! Lift your eyes from your navel to see the stars! When I move from my deep, introverted, self-centeredness to the perspective of the universe, change takes complete and perfect shape. This is a revolutionary way to measure life. I find that my Lord calls me to look at what I can do, and then to do those things that I can. When I reach my limitations I have to accept those boundaries. Under Christ's Lordship I leave to Him the care for those issues that are beyond my reach.

This message, found in the "Prayer for Serenity" has been adapted by Alcoholics Anonymous:

Lord, give me the serenity to accept
   what I cannot change,
The courage to change what can be changed,
And the wisdom to know the difference.
   Amen.

That prays it all! It is as inspired as any prayer ever given. Under the Lordship of Jesus Christ, when I get this message inside me I will do what I can as best I can. What I can't do, I'll not let possess me. I'll use all the wisdom God gives me to distinguish between the two, and I'll let my life rest in the difference. You and I can live with a lot of change when we measure life by these dimensions.

What Counts Most with You?

Let's explore further what it means to "let my life rest" in God's difference. It is very much a part of what happens in Sunday morning worship services; there's a lot of rest in worship services. But it is far more revolutionary than those jokes about sleeping in church!

Worship is a time of getting life into God's perspective, a way of clarifying what has ultimate value. It is the God-given way of finding the rightful place for what is most important to us. As a Christian, my worship must place Jesus Christ at the center of my life and make sure that everything else is revolving around Him. It is the daily or weekly way of making sure that Christ is both first and last with me. By touching base in this way I can relax internally.

The truth is that many of us who go to church really value other things as our ultimate. We say a creed to affirm that Jesus is Lord, but we actually operate with very different priorities. Our real worship may start when we go to work on Monday or look in the mirror before going to bed at night. It is this confusion that keeps many of us in constant turmoil even though we carry some brand of Christian label with us.

Change can eat away at our misplaced values. If the ultimate worth in my life is my children, all that will change as they grow up and move away. If my ultimate hope is for personal security, change is going to erode every fiscal plan I can lay. How can I weigh my values and what change is doing to me? Through worship. Worship is the chance to let God help me rethink my life and discover if I am being undermined.

In my moments of thought, prayer, and listening, I can reframe the whole picture in Jesus Christ. This is truly the final word. I can let change help me rethink where I actually am. Then in my worship I make Christ truly central. When He has become central, you and I can stand anything. We can bear anything. We can hold anything.

The One who is constant is the only pillar I have against the transitory nature of life. He is the only One against whom we can lean as things move and turn. In various ways the Scripture proclaims, "In Christ Jesus we have hope" (Rom. 8:24; 1 Tim. 1:1; Heb. 7:18-22). Our hope is in Jesus Christ the Lord. We find this little phrase popping up throughout the New Testament as a promise of permanence. *He is our hope.*

This hope is the knowledge that there are times when I will be faced with real injustice, when people will deceive me, when I am going to be truly wrong, when I am going to be caught in ambiguities which I can't fathom and yet must decide on. There will be times when I am going to be let down, when I won't even understand what's going on!

But even when I'm fogged in, Christ is still my hope, and that is enough. As I live and struggle with these conditions, I find that no matter what else happens to me, Christ is sufficient. *He* is the center against which every other thing moves.

Who Is Your Doorkeeper?

A friend of mine liked to use the cliche "under the circumstances." When asked for an opinion he would begin, "Well, under the circumstances . . ." One day he shared a new insight: He had come to the new realization as a Christian that he shouldn't be living "under the circumstances." As a Christian he should be living *above* the circumstances! Here is the power and the ability to learn to live with change.

John wrote, "Behold, I have set before you an open door, which no one is able to shut" (Rev. 3:8, *RSV*). I have grounded my life in the certainty that Jesus is the only One who opens and closes doors. All the divine hinges move by Him. I can say to myself, "What comes and what goes can be handled because the Doorkeeper is keeping my going in and my going out from this day forth and forevermore. He will handle it! He will settle it!"

At the start of every day, every week, every year, Christ is opening the door, and no one can close it. No set of circumstances can close what is left with Him. Nothing is inevitable. He is the constant, and all He asks is that I have the courage to go through my circumstances. As I go through them with Him, the changes will take care of themselves.

Strange, but that bandit Change does at times seem to

turn into the doorkeeper! Stranger yet, what first seemed as agitation in the churning place can become creativity. Out of all of the disorientation new perspectives arise. What was disorganizing is used by God to rearrange into better possibilities and patterns. When unmasked, change reveals the face of God!

May I invite you to take whatever in your life is a troubling situation and point it toward the Doorkeeper. Take the unsettledness and undefined fears in hand and clarify what you can't do. Commit yourself to act as you have the opportunity, and to let the rest be settled by whatever doors Christ will open and close for you. Right now decide that all the other issues of change will be settled only on one basis. Let that same voice speak to you, "This is my beloved Son, listen to Him." When everything else is gone and the light has faded, Christ and His purposes will stand.

Some Helps to Wholeness

Try this experiment: For the next 30 days get completely alone and start a dialogue with Jesus. In your secret place start talking to Him as if He were sitting opposite you. Develop a mental image of what He might look like. As you talk, envision Him listening with all His compassionate concern. Share how hard it is to face change. Ask Christ to show you how His eternal nature can give you security. Just let the conversation flow as you would with your best and most intimate friend. Once a day take time out for this talk. The following prayer can help you get started.

Lord Jesus, help me to know and feel how all time flows into your hand. You do hold the speedometer of my life. I will not be afraid of the pace of events, but will rest in the assurance that change is your vehicle of redemption. When I feel panic, take me beneath the surface so that I can again make you central in my life. It is my single intention that nothing but you, Jesus, will be supreme. I now relinquish my control of all my worries to your hands as the Guide to the throttle of my time. (Now you continue with what *you* feel) . . .

For Further Consideration

1. What forms of change bother you the most? What personal experiences of change have been the hardest for you to live through?
2. How do you adjust when changes come? What do you do that is positive and helpful?
3. Can you learn to accept change that is best for others when it causes you conflicts? Can you let your children be free persons? Can you let those of lesser opportunity be your equal?
4. In your true worship, what might compete for first place in your life?
5. How big is your Christ? Is He really bigger than the changes you fear? Are you willing to let Him take you through a new door? Would you let Him change how you see your marriage? Would you let Him change how you spend your spare time? Would you let Him open a whole new door to the future?

6
JEALOUSY
THE GREEN-EYED MONSTER

As I turned on the TV, before me flashed one of those confounding 1940 movies. Immediately, before I could even identify the film, I began to get out of my chair to change the channels. (It was one of those epics in which the girls have big hats, the guys have double-breasted suits and all the actors are walking cliches!)

In this "golden oldie" a 1930 beauty queen was talking to the handsome hero. As I was crossing the room, the dialogue began to take on more than the usual content and I paused to listen. The girl was lamenting her life; it was a failure. She had been married twice and was afraid of being a three-time loser.

In a more touching note, she talked of her love as always turning sour, always becoming shoddy and phony. She feared that there was no alternative for her.

Suddenly she turned on the man across the table and began to pour out her anger. Jealousy had wrecked her life. It had made everything she loved tarnish and turn green.

"Isn't there any kind of medicine? Isn't there anything I can take for that venomous green-eyed monster, jealousy?" Then I changed the channel.

But it struck me that she was really articulating what I have heard in other places, in other words and in other ways. How truly vicious, corrupting and deadly jealousy can be!

A Dragon in Your Head

Jealousy is like a beast lurking beneath our best emotions, waiting for the worst moment to strike. Keith Miller in his book, *Habitation of Dragons*, helped me to understand this. Here he described our subconscious as the murky unknown where we store the monsters of our past. Occasionally one of these sticks up its head, and we lop off what we can see. It submerges again like a Loch Ness mystery, only to return on a new occasion. We have to keep cutting off each new layer that appears in order to seem truly Christian.[1]

I find that one of the most long-necked and most persistent monsters is the green-eyed one. It usually goes unnoticed until its job is done! Sooner or later every one of us feels its bite!

It is no coincidence that in the medieval framework of virtue and vice, envy and jealousy were listed among the seven deadly sins. Medieval minds were very clear on the division between a Christian character and an evil character. They made a careful catalog of what made a person evil. Jealousy and envy are so vicious that they were recognized as being able to ruin anybody. It happens the same way today. The lines of that old

1940's movie can come back to haunt any of us!

I find envy to be one of the especially dangerous booby traps of our times. Just look around us. There are always people who seem to have more, to have it in better quality and have it piled higher and deeper. We just know that if we could have their breaks and opportunities, we could have acquired the same. Envy grows within us and the stage is set—on comes pure personal jealousy disguised as righteous indignation!

The deceptive thing about jealousy is that so often it comes to us in the very best kinds of costumes. We think it is only honest to say, "It isn't fair; they've gotten the break *I* should have had. I have been maligned, unnoticed and unrecognized." In our relationships with friends and acquaintances, we develop an intense resentment. The truth is that we have not been abused or misused; it is just pure jealousy.

You've Been Short-Changed!

Jealousy and prejudices are two sides of the same coin. Prejudice is what I feel toward people who I think are beneath me. Jealousy is what I feel toward people who I think are above me. It's just two sides of the same coin.

On one side is the guy who claims he's not prejudiced. It's just that he doesn't happen to like Poles, or Italians, or whatever! On the other side are people who might say, "I wouldn't be in their place for the world! I wouldn't have that kind of home! I wouldn't have the burden that those expensive cars bring." What they really mean is, "I'd give my soul to get that!"

We are pushed and pulled. This comes out in very nitty-gritty ways when you live with someone. You find yourself giving criticism or being derogatory. You say, "Oh, it's for your own good." What you really mean is

93

that you have intense feelings of jealousy, and that you want to cut that person down to at least one size smaller than you are.

At the moment it feels good and satisfying to squash the object of your envy. Of course, the sad truth is that you are only being infected; you are being diseased by your own jealousy. You can be so engulfed by your green-tinted glasses that the whole world starts looking like an abysmal plot to get you. You may feel very bad about it, but you're stuck with the feeling.

A clinical case study in a pastoral counseling course described a young lady who had been married several times. Each relationship had been ruined by her intense suspicious jealousy. Going back through her life, the counselor discovered an intense sibling rivalry. She had interpreted everyone as liking her sister better. Finally she decided that even her parents loved her older sister more. She developed a pattern in which everyone seemed to have something better going for them.

Many nights she would have a recurring dream that someone was going to take something away from her. It had become pathological with her. At night the chronic jealousy monster emerged, and his devouring, snarling head struck within the person he afflicted.

How Jesus Slays the Jealousy Monster

Remember that great Old Testament story of David's fight with the beasts that attacked him? The monsters were slain in God's name. If David could kill bears and lions with the Lord's help, why can't we fight our internal monsters with the same spiritual support? Jesus intends that we do exactly that.

One particular incident in our Lord's ministry showed the apostles how they could do this very thing. The jealousy monster had badly bitten them and they were fighting over who was the most important in the group. They were spiritually defeated by their internal competitiveness.

"So they came to Capernaum. And when they were indoors he asked them, 'What were you discussing as we came along?' They were silent, for on the way they had been arguing about who should be the greatest. Jesus sat down and called the twelve, and said to them, 'If any man wants to be first, he must be last and servant of all.' Then he took a little child and stood in front of them all, and putting his arms around him, said to them, 'Anyone who welcomes one little child like this for my sake is welcoming me. And the man who welcomes me is welcoming not only me but the one who sent me!' " (Mark 9:33-37, *Phillips*).

The path to victory is in being the servant of all. The unpretentiousness of the little child was to be the disciples' example. What an irony! Strength comes from what seems to be weakness.

Anyone who welcomes a child in this manner welcomes the Father. This is the clue to the way out of the insane jealousy that would devour us. If we would be free, we must discover how to successfully be last. This strategy of cutting down others must stop. In contrast, our task is to lift people up.

So here's the question: "How can I employ all the power of Jesus Christ to really kill my own personal dragon of jealousy?"

Where Monsters Are Born

Let's explore how I become jealous. Why is it I am an envious creature? It is natural for me to see things I wish I had, to see in others qualities I would like to have in myself. That's normal! It's normal to want something better. But jealousy starts on a different basis. Out of a natural desire for betterment, I begin to form a resentment. Resentment is the mother of jealousy.

Every day of the week I experience many things that could be a source of resentment. Someone gets recognition I feel I should have received. Someone seems to be appreciated in a way that I felt I deserved instead. Moreover, I am right about it! Often others *do* get breaks that should have been mine.

When things haven't been going my way, I naturally have feelings about them. But when I let these feelings evolve into a resentment that is attached to a person, then I am on my way to being ambushed by jealousy. I must stop these feelings back at the point of the resentment. I can't help the fact that I have feelings, but I certainly can prevent those feelings from developing and attaching themselves to the other person. If I do not discipline myself, the venomous poison of resentment will begin to do its work.

When jealousy becomes a chronic problem that persists in my life, I have to look for something deeper than the situation at hand—a larger beast lurking behind the immediate issue. It has been found, clinically, that jealousy has its roots in two particular directions. First, deeply rooted in our past is a need to be loved. Second, this need is compounded by our deprivation of love.

Every one of us must be loved, affirmed and recognized. When we are denied these needs, an off-color veil is draped over our whole interpretation of life. Some very strange behavior can come from a simple need for honest, emotional recognition. Accidents, illnesses, and seemingly unrelated problems can begin to well up in us out of a desire to be confirmed and loved. When this need is frustrated deep within a small child, the real breeding ground for the monsters of the future is open for business.

A child interprets life by his fear that he is not truly loved and affirmed, and this fear spills over into many, many other areas.

Quite often I hear the residue of deprivation spill over in discussions about personal salvation. "Being saved" is a theological term for an assurance we have about a personal relationship with God in Jesus Christ that holds us secure into eternity. In discussing this with people they have said to me, "I really can't believe God loves me in any way that would be permanent."

They have a difficult time emotionally seeing God as being eternally concerned for them. They haven't discovered that the real God is hidden behind a mosaic made up of the parents and authority figures of their past. Consequently, He doesn't seem any more dependable than these authority figures were.

We can argue the problem scripturally, but the actual difficulty is in their own "habitation of dragons." Behind their questions lurks a fear of themselves as people who can be truly and completely loved. These unresolved doubts make them a walking target for jealousy. Fear can take over, controlling and ruining their lives.

In the words of Victor Hugo, "The supreme happiness of life is to know that you are loved." Not only is this true, but it has profound implications for our personal theology. A supreme sense of well-being and happiness is tied to the conviction that we are really loved by God.

God Thinks You're First Class!

You are loved and valuable. Jesus Christ says so! That is the message we preach as the ultimate answer to life's insecurities. The gospel is a statement about our value; we must learn to appropriate this judgment of Jesus in our innermost being.

If jealousy is a problem for you, one of the clues that you must find on the deepest level of your being is that you truly are a loved person regardless of any other circumstances. You must learn to quit evaluating your worth and importance by what is socially fed back to you. Let it be settled with God. You have the final stamp of approval in Jesus Christ. That's enough. Let it emotionally complete you.

How can you experience this emotional completion? Let's return to that story of the apostles and Jesus. There is great significance when Jesus takes the little child and sets him in the midst of them with the observation, "Here is an example of what I am talking about. If you want to see a true perspective on importance, look at the way in which a child tends to see himself" (see Mark 9:35-37).

Here is something that only Jesus could have seen with His perceptive eyes. Every one of us has a little child living within us. This child of our past is very real, very alive and very vital. He needs the touch of Jesus, just as that Capernaum lad needed it that day he met Jesus.

The Child of Your Past

We can't explore all the ramifications and possibilities of the child of our past, but the idea is further elaborated in Dr. Thomas Harris's popular book on transactional analysis, "I'm O.K., You're O.K." [2] Dr. Harris describes how in very young childhood we all develop a whole set of mental tape recordings of our perceptions of life.

Our mental tape recorder ran 24 hours a day. Everything that happened around us and to us went into that tape recorder and was totally absorbed as the final measuring stick for the future. These tapes are stored in our heads as indelible messages about reality. Today memories are replayed unconsciously as if they are still final reality.

No matter who we are or what our experiences have been, as a child we picked up a whole set of ideas, attitudes and feelings which unconsciouly affect everything that happens to us on a feeling level today. This, says Harris, is the little child within us.

This little child develops a particular stance toward life and a unique position toward reality. Harris feels most of us have a "not O.K. child" tape in us. This tiny person was so small that, in looking at the great big adults in the land of giants, he developed a permanent sense of insecurity. It was only natural to feel that whatever these giants said and did was right! They were so big and powerful.

It's hard for us to remember what it was like to stand next to a chair that hit us at eye level. Can you feel again what a bed was like when it seemed as big as a swimming pool? Whatever the giants did could make you feel very small.

Because of feeling so small, all of us, to some extent, have developed feelings of inadequacy. We are not whole; our opinions don't "feel" entirely valid; other people seem better. So we all have a greater need for love and affirmation that we are constantly carrying with us.

Here's the clincher. Sometimes, situations that threaten or challenge us reach right through this present moment and back to the center of our past. These experiences hook into those tapes of yesterday and we begin filtering today's situations through the memories of yesterday.

That is why present events cause us to react as if we were three or four years old. Have you noticed how you and your wife can sound like four-year-olds when you really start bickering? You say things to each other that are *incredible!*

"You're a dirty rat!"

"Why don't you drop dead!"

"I hate you!"

You find yourself saying these things because they "just come out." When there is a "not O.K. child" living in you and it gets stepped on, all those "I'm not loved enough" feelings come to the surface.

Put on a New Record

It is at this point that the gospel of Jesus Christ must infiltrate into our innermost beings. There are at least two ways in which the gospel can do this.

First, Dr. Harris has discovered that we can develop a whole new set of tape recordings out of our present moment. Psychologically, we can make decisions that etch new possibilities in our lives.

This affords me a powerful breakthrough! A new mental recording is made as I make a faith decision and receive God's love that has already been given to me. What a new beginning this has been in my life! No matter what I tend to feel intuitively, God's affirmation of me is certain.

It is a great step forward in personal maturity when you learn not to evaluate the present moment by feelings alone. People may make you mad, but this can be a very incomplete grasp of the situation. Someone may make you feel very exhilarated, yet they could be just manipulating you.

A mature perspective goes beyond feeling and seeks the objective truth in Jesus Christ. I have been affirmed by Him! I am loved and I am O.K. in Him. That's what I'll go with. I must make new internal tapes that will restore trust to the "child" within me.

On a second front, I need to have some of those old tapes erased by the Holy Spirit's power. That erasing can happen if the child of yesterday is touched. I need to feel the little child within me literally held in the arms of Christ.

Perhaps it sounds strange for me to write like that. Isn't yesterday already gone and past? Let's remember that time is always in the "now" before God. Every moment is a present one. He sees the past and the future all as right now. So, He can reach into my yesterday as easily as He can touch my today.

To help me envision this, I see the Father's loving hand holding that little child of my past. With this vision, I can do my best to change my own reservations.

When I begin to doubt, to feel the apprehensions of the past creeping back in, I recall the fact of this experience. I let my new memory settle the issue. When I have reached the limits of what I can do, I remember that the Holy Spirit is ready to reach beyond my limits of self-assertion and finish the job for me.

One cold, winter evening this fell together for me in a powerful life-changing way. I had invited Rosalind Rinker to speak at a special Congregational meeting. Rosalind is well known for her ability to lead people into a personal encounter with the extraordinary possibilities of prayer. On this special evening she led me to new discoveries of what can happen when self and Spirit hit head-on.

After sharing some of her exciting insights into the value of praying, this former missionary to China asked us to experiment in silence. We began by quietly getting in touch with the Holy Spirit. Prayerfully we "tuned in" to God's presence. As we prayed, Rosalind reminded us that the Holy Spirit's reach is timeless. He goes backward into our past needs as easily as forward into tomorrow. Now we are ready to get in touch with ourselves.

She asked me to envision this child of my past. As I prayed, I asked God to help me reexperience my childhood, and at the same moment I tried to remember and imagine how it was.

Suddenly I could see myself in my mind's eye at about eight years of age. I was startled to discover that I was walking across a school playground. Once again it was a Saturday night and I was walking across that playground in the dark. It was very frightening. I began to see how burdened that little child was. That little boy seemed very troubled. As I looked closer, he had a large pack on his back.

Then Rosalind directed me further: "I want you to see Jesus Christ entering the scene. Look! He's standing next to you!"

By the power of the Spirit I could see Him there. Roz then said, "Now I want you to watch carefully. Jesus Christ is going to reach out and touch this child. He is going to heal whatever exists in that child."

Immediately the Master's hand reached out, just as He had picked up the child in Capernaum. As He touched me, that big knapsack burden on my little child's back was gone!

It was so physically real that I found myself spontaneously rising off the seat. The moment was over! That "lifting up" had just jarred me awake. But in that moment I knew that a very "not O.K. child" had received the touch of divine "O.K.-ness," and I sat there amazed and hushed in awe.

The Holy Spirit had blended a depressing part of yesterday into the prayerful opportunities of today. It was almost too much to talk about, except that I began to breathe more deeply and fully than I had ever thought possible.

My nostrils were filled with the joy of a new rarefied air of God's breath. A new wholeness had come to Robert Wise. He was all right. He was O.K. He was approved.

Why Not You?

It can happen to you. In fact, Jesus Christ is even more anxious to love that child of yours than you are to have the child made whole. That's how complete and encompassing His love is. Why not carve out some time to practice this kind of meditation? Get in touch with Christ. Get in touch with yourself. Then just be open to whatever Christ wants to do in and for you.

Here's another suggestion on letting your life be made complete. Jesus has a strategy when He says, "You must be a servant." When I look at the world and feel I ought to be first, to be recognized, this tells me that the perspective I need is to reverse my tendencies. Just the act of helping someone else is an exercise in becoming whole. Stop focusing attention on yourself and instead aim at someone else's needs, and you will begin to break out of your own bondage.

If you find someone for whom you have jealousy, a deep sense of envy or a biting sense of resentment, here is the next step in release: Sit down and figure out all the things that ought to happen to you or be yours out of that relationship. Enumerate all the things you feel you've really got coming. Write out what hasn't been fair, noting the sources of jealousy. Then decide what you think that other person really ought to do for you to make things right.

Once you've clarified this, in the name of Christ decide to reverse the arrangement! Decide that *you* will do all the loving things for that person!

This may be very painful, very difficult emotionally,

but as you persevere you are going to be really changed. I will give you a money-back guarantee that if you will do for the other person what you feel should be done for you, you will heal the jealous relationship permanently. Jesus sealed this truth with His own promise, "The first shall be last, and the last will finally be first." (See Matt. 19:30.) Think it over—this promise carries God's guarantee of fulfillment!

The person who wants to be whole has to be like a child, with spontaneous, alive, unencumbered openness. If you receive Christ and His words like that, He says you will receive the Father. To receive the Father is to receive His life-changing and rearranging power. I invite you in the name of Christ to a new wholeness that you have never known. Let it happen on that level of the little child living within you. As you do, the green-eyed monster in your life will perhaps submerge for the last time. He can be destroyed only by the One who walks above waters and heals all storms.

Some Helps to Wholeness

Have you been "praying your way" through these chapters? I hope so. The answers for your life aren't in new insights so much as in new actions. Acting on these directions in prayer is one of the most powerful therapeutic activities possible. Why not wrestle with your dragon this way?

Dear Father, I know you are my ultimate parent. Somehow along the way I have picked up burdens and difficulties you did not intend. I have developed feelings and fears that you do not want me to have. Now I want to get things back into the right perspective. I want to open myself to you, so that you can reach completely behind my facades to the real center.

Please plant the image of Jesus Christ there and nurture that Presence forever in me. Make me so sure of your love that I can face all of my own personal unsureness and dismiss the fears of yesterday. Always through Jesus Christ. Amen.

For Further Consideration

1. What makes you jealous? Do you really know why you feel that way?
2. Has jealousy ever ruined relationships or opportunities for you? List some. Be specific.
3. It's hard to face up to feelings of not being loved. Have you ever wanted someone to affirm you, but the opposite happened? What did it do to you?
4. What happens to you when your fear of rejection takes over? Has it surprised you? What clues are here for the way your "child" feels? Write down some specific recent emotional reactions to situations in which you felt rejection. Trace these outbursts back into your childhood. What do they tell you?
5. Try this exercise for experiencing Christ's presence. Dare to pray it through to the center of your life.
6. Write out how you might reverse a relationship. In Christ's name resolve to follow it through.

Footnotes

1. Keith Miller, *Habitation of Dragons* (Waco, Texas: Word Books, 1970).
2. Thomas A Harris, *I'm O.K., You're O.K.* (Old Tappan, New Jersey: Fleming H. Revell Co., 1967).

7
ANXIETY
THE GNAWING DEVOURER

Few of us will ever come within striking distance of a shark, yet the movie *Jaws* was so convincing that it caused millions of people to look twice before they jumped into a swimming pool! They could feel the horrifying possibility of being eaten alive. Of course, *Jaws* wasn't real. All that terror was created by an incredible mechanical monster. There is, however, a beast that is very real and as deadly as any shark. This stalker is likely to catch up with us at any moment of the day. It is a gnawing devourer that can eat us alive. It chews up and digests our best energies, best feelings and best attitudes.

This beast is called anxiety!

Anxiety comes unannounced and is prepared to stay beyond any limits of invitation. It feeds on our imagination and is entertained by our fears. Anxiety is so common that most of the time we don't distinguish it from our more healthy feelings. Yet it has taken a tool of human life far beyond what any beasts of the deep have ever accomplished.

Contrast the ever-present reality of anxiety with what the Scriptures have to say. The apostle Paul writes, "Have no anxiety about anything, but in everything by prayer and supplication with thanksgiving let your requests be made known to God. And the peace of God, which passes all understanding, will keep your hearts and your minds in Christ Jesus" (Phil. 4:6, *RSV*). Did you get that? Have no anxiety about anything!

This seems impossible in the age in which we live. How can we be free from anxiety with the pressures that you and I face? What about competitiveness and the intensity of life? How can we not have anxiety about these things? Philippians 4:6 must have been for somebody else, or at least for some other age! We live in the pressure cooker of competition and tension every day of our lives.

Recently a popular magazine had an interesting article about what happens to children through Little League athletics. The writer was raising questions about whether Little League baseball and football is good for kids since parents create tremendous tension and anxiety for their children. I did some coaching in juvenile football for one year. I found I couldn't endure any more than that! If our kids don't excel to their parents' expectations, anxiety is poured into them through the unrealistic demands and feverish urging of the "fans."

In Cub Scouts we had a project called Pinewood Derby Racers. Every kid got a block of wood which he was supposed to take home and whittle into a racing car. Then the families would have races. Before long I discovered that this too was really for the parents. One man took his boy down to the University of Oklahoma and had a professor of structural engineering design the car for him!

On the night of the races I was picked to judge the winning cars as they came across the finish line. I had mothers chewing me out for a week! You had better believe that anxiety is part of these times!

In the midst of all this, Jesus has given us some instruction that only seems to increase the problem. He said that we are to love the unlovable. There is tremendous tension in that too! Have you ever tried returning love for hate? We are to be found working with the hungry and the dispossessed. In fact, the whole nature of the Christian life sounds like an anxiety-ridden experience. Yet in the midst of all this the apostle Paul says that we are not to live anxiety-filled lives!

Paul's Answer to Anxiety

Let's attack the problem as we have in the preceding chapters, by applying biblical truth in a psychological way. It's not enough to say that the Bible is true; it is meant to be our *personal experience*. The abundant life in Christ is not just a future promise—it can be an ever-present reality! The abundant life ought to be true for each one of us all the time (see John 10:10).

Unfortunately, all too often we who are believers fail to live out consistently the emotional power of the gospel message. Too many of us have been theologically accurate and scripturally sound all our lives but have not been emotionally appropriating the promise in Christ's message. My purpose in this book is to uncover some of the insights that will free us to be the full people God wants us to be.

God's emphasis is on what you can be! Christian faith isn't a *word game*; it is a *power performance*. That's why there is an important difference between the Christian faith and any other philosophy or religion. With Christianity it is not enough to know that "the faith" is true; this is only a starting point. The Christian faith is not intended to be primarily a *philosophy* but a *behavior.*

Its power is given only to those who actually *live* it. All the promises and all the help become ours only as the message is synthesized into our behavior. The value of what I am writing comes not by saying, "I believe that's true," but by *making it your own experience.* Read these pages over and over until you see clearly what you actually need to do!

The release of Christ's power is in doing; His promise is that our faith offers self-sufficiency in the midst of adversity. You *can* enjoy self-sufficiency, and you *can* live above the nagging influence of anxiety!

In 2 Corinthians 4, Paul enumerates some of the conditions in his own life that had been sources of painful difficulty: "We have this treasure [speaking of the Christian life and gospel] in earthern vessels, to show that the transcendent power belongs to God and not to us. We are afflicted in every way, but not crushed; perplexed, but not driven to despair; persecuted, but not forsaken; struck down, but not destroyed; always carrying in the body the death of Jesus, so that the life of Jesus may also be manifest in our bodies" (2 Cor. 4:7-10, *RSV*).

When we understand that we are earthen vessels carrying the death of Christ within us, then we can begin to see what His life brings forth. Again, here is the theme from previous chapters. In dying to life, we find it. It is true that, in seeking first the Kingdom of God, "all these things" will be added unto us emotionally.

We can't avoid problems; there will always be times when we will be knocked down, persecuted or afflicted. But in the face of this we need not be anxious, distraught, destroyed or forsaken. Anxiety has no right to gnaw on us; God's promise is that we can live far beyond the reach of this devourer!

Look Anxiety in the Eye

Let's understand the role of the devourer so that we can get anxiety in perspective. As we understand how we function, we are better able to apply what Christ promises. Let me assure you that it is OK to face up to any emotions you feel. Don't ever hide from yourself.

The Christian community has had a problem with openness. We read in the Bible that it is bad to be angry, to lust and to hate (see Matt. 5:21-48). It is clear that these are not constructive feelings. Because we want to obey Scripture, we may try to suppress the reality of these emotions when they occur.

But denial is destructive! Whatever we feel, we feel. Our experience has validity whether it is profitable or not. So we must develop the habit of being completely honest with ourselves. We must recognize these things that boil to the surface, and we must put the right name on what we feel.

Does this sound confusing? It might, since we know that some of these emotional eruptions are very destructive to others and to ourselves. How can I be honest with myself about my feelings while at the same time recognizing that these very emotions are unchristian?

Let's think about this with a couple of emotions that can create considerable anxiety for everyone.

Anxiety is the result of internal confusion. When we are uncertain or confused we feel anxious. Often this emotional turmoil is a secondary result that comes as a spin-off of another emotion. The original feeling gets displaced, and we lose touch with our principle apprehension. We're not sure exactly what's wrong, but we

111

feel upset. Anger and fear are particularly devastating when we fail to face them honestly.

Anger can be a powerful undercurrent that stirs up anxiety. If I vent my anger I may do some very harmful things to those around me. But I can't *deny* that I'm angry without turning the anger inward on myself. And anger turned inward becomes the substance of depression. I can't escape the fire in my stomach; to let it smolder is to burn myself and to become victimized by an unnecessary anxiety born of my own hostility.

So what do I do about this? I keep from putting labels on my emotions until after I have fully faced them! Good or bad doesn't count until I can honestly be in touch with what's happening inside my churning place. I must recognize what I am feeling whenever it hits and I must face it fully. I can't bring the power of Christ to bear on my life until I open myself to the real place it must work. Then both my anger and the anxiety it causes can be attacked by God's power.

Fear has the same potential for creating chaos, yet it has an important place in my life. Fear is a very valid emotion, for it is a barometer that warns me of danger. Fright causes me to think about things in my life which may require adjustment. I must sort through and find appropriate responses to those things that could be destructive.

But what if we lose perspective on our fears? Then anxiety is born! When we fail to look our fears in the eye, we are captured by their consequences.

Look at the relationship between fear and anxiety. Fear always has an object; you know where there is something of which you are afraid; you can pinpoint a valid reason for your concern. Anxiety, on the other hand, is nameless. There is no object for its apprehension; all perspective has been lost.

112

Anxiety is like a strange animal inside us that moves in all directions but has no center. This devourer roams aimlessly across our every concern, contaminating all he touches. His journey seems to have no purpose but to make us miserable. In the end we are completely defeated because of his nameless, directionless churning.

Look anxiety in the eye! Face the facts! Before you decide on the good or the bad, get the basics of your concern in sight. When you hide the truth from yourself, you will find it impossible to defeat anxiety. But when you confront your fears you allow the Holy Spirit to deal with the real issues of your life, and this is where anxiety is starved to death!

Courage Begins with Fear

Recognizing fear makes courage possible. I once thought that courage is the ability to fear nothing, that courageous people simply had no fears. But I have discovered just the opposite. If you never fear, this is not a sign of courage but of dullness.

I was watching a motorcyclist race madly on our hills. Was he courageous? I think he was stupid! Without a helmet he was taking chances that could kill or impair him for the rest of his life. True courage starts with my fears and all the realism possible. I recognize how deadly the consequences may be, but in the face of that I still act.

I like the way Joanna Ballie put it: "The plagued man is not the man who feels no fear, for that's stupid and irrational, but he whose noble soul fears subdue and bravely bears the danger that nature shrinks from."[1] This is the man who bravely dares what he knows can be deadly. His courageous fear bears no resemblance to the pale anxiety of the chronic worrier.

In Herman Melville's classic novel *Moby Dick*, a sail-

or called Starbuck commanded one of the whaling boats. He would say, "I want no man in my boat who is not afraid."[2] Fear is a sign of intelligence!

One of my childhood heroes was a cousin who was decorated for bravery under fire during World War II. I was sure he was the bravest man in the world, for Jack came back with a silver and a bronze star. In my childish, awed way I remember asking him, "How could you do this tremendous thing?" His response was, "I was scared to death! But I did it in spite of my fear." That is true courage!

As I separate fear from anxiety, the Scriptures call me to absolute realism. I am called to look right in the face of what life gives me and recognize it for what it is. My anxiety and anguish come from failing to recognize the true object of many of my fears. When I fail to face the truth of my fear, I get myself caught in that nameless, churning circle.

Already I've learned that I can face life, not by retreating or escaping, but by approaching it head-on. I am to look at whatever is before me and courageously recognize it as being part of God's opportunity. I become unrealistic when I deny the inevitable. Anxiety is born when I start to think I can't accept life if my fears come to pass.

But a powerful release occurs when I look this fear in the face and know that God can use even what seems impossible to me. I can look anything right in the eye and believe that even disaster can be God's opportunity. I will accept it as that.

This makes an enormous difference! Whatever has befallen you, see it for what it is and know it as God's opportunity. There it becomes true courage.

How does this put anguish and anxiety in perspective? First of all, I recognize true fear and clarify it. I must recognize where my real, honest fears ought to be placed.

Second, I must be willing to take whatever action is necessary in order to deal with the problem. In the name of Christ I must be willing to take whatever action needs to be taken to deal with the problem. In the name of Christ I must be willing to do what I can do to resolve the issues.

Surely this sounds like plain common sense. Yet it comes from hours of counseling experience with people who only *talked* about their problems. After the resolution was clear they would say, "OK, what's next?" They would ignore the true solution and start searching for easier, less demanding solutions!

When they returned, it was with new anguish. They would say, "I don't know what to do!"

My response would be, "Well, I thought we were going to act."

They would respond, "I was afraid you'd say that!"

It's true. It's inescapable. We begin to deal with anxiety when in Christ's name we see it as an opportunity and then act on the difficult things in our lives.

You're Not Atlas!

Now let's look at the other extreme. In 2 Corinthians 4:7-10 the apostle Paul wants us to see that, as life comes to us, we subtly begin to believe it all depends on us! Rather than running, we try to carry it all.

This is particularly true with difficult problems. We really believe that we have to carry them all on our shoulders. I've done it many times. The whole world is my problem; I feel convinced I am an indispensable, irreplaceable part; it's up to me to hold all the pieces together.

Of course it's overwhelming if I go through life feeling

that if I personally don't do it all, it just can't happen! Does this sound like you? If so, let me suggest a couple of things.

The first is a practical exercise. Every morning get a bucket and fill it full of water. Set it on the counter, and just before you go to work place your fist in that bucket. Pull it out very quickly and observe the hole that you leave. See what happens to the place where your fist was! You'll soon get properly related to the actual scheme of things in life. You'll understand what the Apostle meant when he said, "We have this treasure in earthen vessels, to show that the transcendent power belongs to God and not to us" (2 Cor. 4:7, *RSV*). The apostle Paul, important as he was, was willing to say that he was not indispensable. He was limited and finite; he could not carry it all on his own shoulders.

I must learn to recognize my limitations, and that my only sufficiency in life is from a transcendent power beyond me. Something tremendously important happens to a person when he sees that "it really depends on God."

We carry tremendous anxieties because we believe that everything depends on us, and we don't know what to do about this overwhelming responsibility.

Often I really don't know what to do, yet when I realize how limited I am, how finite I am, how insufficient I am, I am on my way to the larger answer. I just don't leave a hole in that bucket of water! My wet hand teaches me that there is a transcendent power that carries me when I am knocked down, perplexed or pushed up against life's problems. Adversity is God's opportunity! "Don't worry over anything whatever; tell God every detail of your needs in earnest and thankful prayer, and the peace of God, which transcends human understanding, will keep constant guard over your hearts and minds as they rest in Christ Jesus" (Phil. 4:6,7, *Phillips*).

These words so pregnant with promise aren't pie in the sky given for the benefit of hermits who are shut off from the real world of stress and strain. They are meant for people who have come to the end of the rope. When Paul advises not to worry about anything, he is writing to you at the very point of personal problems that seem beyond solution.

Pour your anxieties into your relationship with the heavenly Father. Learn to shift the load into His arms. As you make that transaction, wait for Him to give back peace in exchange for distress.

Let's say more about the effect of anxiety. Make no mistake about it—the physical effect of anxiety is staggering. I had a counselee tell me that her dentist said anxiety was destroying her teeth! This agrees with a medical report which describes how human tissue is broken down and torn apart by anxiety. Anxiety literally gnaws and destroys us internally!

Another study suggested that *100 percent* of fatigue felt by people in sedentary occupations and in good health is emotional fatigue! If as a desk worker you find yourself utterly wrung out by the day's end, it's not the work but the result of the subtle nibbling of anxiety hour by hour. The traffic and the freeways will do the same thing; they physically gnaw away at us unless we learn how to handle them.

Your Two Secret Needs

A modern therapist, Dr. William Glasser, has applied this principle to a whole counseling system. I believe Dr. Glasser has done a unique thing in "reality therapy." His reality therapy embodies the same concepts Jesus used with people (though Dr. Glasser himself does not

117

make this claim). Dr. Glasser has recognized how anxiety causes people to deny some particular facet of reality. When people are under suspicion and anxiety, life becomes unrealistic. As a result, they begin to act in unrealistic ways. All sorts of deteriorating behavior then follows.[3]

Glasser discovered that every one of us has two fundamental needs: relatedness and respect. To handle life appropriately, I must have a certain relatedness with other people, and in turn I must receive respect from them. If I don't receive this, I will not be able to deal with anxiety appropriately. So Glasser teaches people to be realistic and to relate to others with respect. With this kind of help the most serious kinds of problems can be healed!

If the apostle Paul had heard this he would have said "Hallelujah! Praise the Lord! I understand that! That's my way of life." If there was ever a realist, it was Paul.

When asked about the stoning of Stephen, Paul said, "I was there and I held the cloaks. I held their clothes and I was a part of the stoning" (see Acts 7:54-60).

What a man Paul was! Realistically, honestly, he faced up to his past actions. But then he went a step further—he lived the secret of relatedness and respect.

There are always going to be people in this world who do not love us. Many do not even *like* us. And that's hard to accept, since I want everybody to like me. (Why not? I'm such a charming person! Really, isn't that the way you feel, too?)

But the truth is that there are going to be times, many times, when this won't happen. So the Apostle's answer to this problem was, "Love is patient and kind; love is not jealous or boastful; it is not arrogant or rude" (1 Cor. 13:4, *RSV*). Paul teaches me that love is not what I get from people; instead, love is what I give to people re-

118

gardless of what they give to me. Paul could go through life prepared to receive what was being given to him. He would give back love regardless.

Something transforming happens to you when you return love for hate, good for evil, kindness for reviling. You begin to have a powerful feeling of self-respect. You begin to have a feeling of worthwhileness and relatedness which you never had before.

Paul learned how to deal with the effects of anxiety. Whether struck down or in jail, he gave back hope for fear. A powerful vitality and wholeness flowed from him. He pioneered the right to his claim: You don't have to be anxious about anything!

Returning love for hate is hard to learn, and so is practicing affirmation instead of anxiety. But it will add increased measure to everything in your life, especially your emotional health.

Pick the Right Battlefield

There is another dimension to Paul's answer. The physical environment of the problem is really secondary; the problem must always be first dealt with as a *spiritual* issue. You almost wouldn't expect this attitude from someone whose distresses had been so physical!

Go back and read Paul's life story. Thirty-nine times he had been beaten, and he had been chained and in shipwrecks (see 2 Cor. 11:23-29). It was when Paul was in terrible straits, jailed, facing death, and with an inhuman Caesar on the throne that he said, "Don't be anxious!"

Paul knew that these problems weren't the basic issues, for problems are never the final battleground. The Apostle had discovered that the *real* battleground is the spiritual one. "Don't be anxious, but take this to God in prayer and make supplication about it."

119

Before you can deal with whatever is happening to you or is being done to you, you must first decide to accept God's verdict on the matter. You must win this battle spiritually before you can deal with it in the physical realm. So the Apostle suggests to us a method of withdrawing, of getting away from it. Previous to interacting with the source of your anxiety, settle the matter in prayer with God. Granted, getting the peace through prayer is not always easy to do!

Someone has injured me! Someone did something frightening to me! Something destructive lies before me! Something is giving me a nameless gnawing! What shall I do? I must get alone and in prayer struggle with God about this thing. After I have settled it there, then I can walk forward and solve the problem.

Martin Luther, while busy reforming the church, would get up at four or five o'clock every morning and pray for four and five hours a day. John Wesley maintained prayer every morning between five and seven o'clock. We who live in a time of increased mobility and pressure spend five minutes in prayer before we go to sleep, if we're lucky!

I'm suggesting to you that your plan of action is simple. You must get alone and spend whatever time is necessary until the battle has been won in private. Then there will be nothing that you will not be able to handle in public. Though struck down, perplexed at points, and even persecuted, Paul says, "That's all right. Being down is never final. It's the pause before God that helps you win." His is the transcendent power.

Where Does Your Imagination Live?

Paul says to us, "If you believe in goodness and if you value the approval of God, fix your minds on whatever is true and honorable and just and pure and lovely and

120

admirable. Model your conduct on what you have learned from me, on what I have told you and shown you, and you will find that the God of peace will be with you" (Phil. 4:8,9, *Phillips*).

In order to win the battle, fix your mind on the just, the pure, the lovely, and the praiseworthy. You'll find that you don't have time to worry about anything. In prayer and supplication your needs have already been met!

Some Helps to Wholeness

Have you noticed that I keep suggesting that you pray about these problems and answers? This is because I have a conviction born out of my experience that prayer will truly change things.

If you haven't found all this to be as easy as I describe, don't be surprised! How easy is it for you to develop a new in-depth relationship with *anyone*? Sure it's hard! Sure it takes time! How many hours have you spent so far in talking with God? Well, how many minutes, then? There is no shortcut. When you put in the time seeking Him, you'll find I'm right!

Gracious Father, we are thankful for the answer that is at hand. I do not want to put in the time necessary to make it my answer. Help me find the sufficiency that you give to face all of life's adversities. Allow me to decipher the difference between my restless anxieties and my reasonable fears. Help me to deal with what must be done and to be decisive. When I am surrounded by uncertainty, grant me the faith to see you, using these circumstances that are so frightening to me. Help me to go on with my mind fixed on the pure, the just, the good, the praiseworthy, to

121

know that you have set up a constant guard on
the issues that come forth from my heart. In
Christ's name. Amen.

For Further Consideration

1. What creates anxiety in you? Can you find the real
   sources from which this springs?
2. Why and how do we deny our feelings and emotions?
   Do you ever label anger as "just upset"? Is "being
   concerned" your expression for fear? Do you use
   nice names for bad feelings?
3. Do you believe you really leave a hole when you try
   the bucket experiment? Can you take yourself *less*
   seriously? How?
4. What is the meaning of facing up to things realistically and then returning love for rejection?
5. Read Philippians 4:8,9 and see how it can be applied
   to your life.

Footnotes

1. Kate Louise Roberts, comp., *Hoyte's New Encyclopedia of Practical Quotations*
(New York: Funk & Wagnalls Pub. Co., 1940).
2. Herman Melville, *Moby Dick; or the Whale*, Great Books of the Western World
(Chicago: Encyclopedia Britannica, 1952).
3. William Glasser, *Reality Therapy* (New York: Harper & Row, 1965).

8
A FINAL
KISS FROM CHRIST

It is possible to face anything through the power of Christ! Every emotion and every need has a response in His grace. The preceding pages have applied that conviction to specific personal problems. Before we leave we need a final word on a host of other needs that space has not allowed us to explore in depth. Let's see how we can still live abundantly in the last half of the twentieth century.

None of us can avoid the valleys that happen in our lives. It is the Christ style of life that equips me for whatever is going to happen.

The Christian faith never promises to remove me from conflict. Instead, it promises to make me adequate in the midst of my life right now. As I encounter emotional problems that are difficult, I can respond with the lift Christ gives. Hope is the possibility given to me in the touch of Christ!

There is a magnificent liberation in Christ's empowerment. We are a people born out of the extension of His freedom. Such liberation is even intoxication. We had a new wave of this type of vitality sweep the country in the 60's.

We began to dress differently. Clothes were very buoyant, had loud colors and clacking designs. All these external signs reflected what was going on internally. Socially we felt a new freedom, and even our music began to reflect it. Bob Dylan wrote "Blowing in the Wind" to express this new freedom of the spirit. Enormous creativity was blowing in the wind.

This exhilarating freedom caught on with the man in the pew. A whole new spirit blew through the church. I am convinced it was of God. Staid traditional form gave way to spontaneous expression. Routine dullness was broken by fresh creativity. Though there was lots of "fallout," many people "fell in" for the first time! Many got involved in church after years of indifference to traditional, dusty rituals which they had rejected as children.

By the end of the 60's we began to talk about the "emerging church," a new variety of worship and witness in America. Here was a church struggling to be honest, to be real, to be free, to be what it really was. This new style of churchmanship was an attempt to be what God intended His Church to be.

It is summarized in one word: Authentic! If anything ought to characterize the church, it must be this note of authenticity. Wearing a spiritual front is no longer acceptable. Artificial churchmanship just isn't working for people anymore. We are learning to quit kidding ourselves with phony life-styles.

The True Christ-Style

This new institutional embodiment of realness can be called the Christ-style. The Christ-style is a way of liberation and authenticity. When we began to pick this up we were returning to exactly the thing that Jesus had said in the beginning. He advised the Jews, "If you continue in my word, you are truly my disciples, and you will know the truth, and the truth will make you free" (John 8:31,32, *RSV*). We have discovered again Christ's truth makes us free!

When Christ first taught this, His hearers' response was, "We were never in bondage." But Jesus replied, "Then you don't even begin to know how much captivity you have been in!" (See John 8:33-40.)

How would we welcome Jesus' words in our twentieth century? If Christ confronted us with the message that we are a captured people, would we hear it any more clearly? Or would we say, "What's He talking about? I need to be free? I've never been in bondage to anybody!"

Jesus replies, "Yes, but you don't know how 'hung up' you can be, how much bondage your life has. Look at your own emotional handcuffs!"

Deep down inside we know He's right. We are bound to unnamed fears, unfilled needs, frustrated ambitions, and hopes that have turned empty. We would very much like to be the authentic, free people who live with a zest for life.

And Jesus responds to our need! "If you continue in my words, if you go in that direction, the truth will make you free, and then you will be free indeed. My words are the key to my life-style. It is in my commands that you will find your dreams fulfilled."

Let's look a bit harder at this freedom, this liberation that comes from God's Word. We are promised that if we continue in the Word, it will make us the authentic people that God insists we must become. No matter what life brings or what emotional difficulty we are confronted with, we can be liberated to be what the Holy Spirit would create. The Bible promises this. Great literature demonstrates it.

Jesus and Our Jails

One of my favorite books is Fyodor Dostoyevsky's *The Brothers Karamozov*,[1] one of the great, all-time classics. Dostoyevsky tells an imaginary story of the Inquisition in Seville, Spain. In the midst of the Inquisition Christ comes back again. Let me paraphrase this story for you.

Men with probing minds and courageous questions are being hauled before the bar of the Inquisition. Those whose length and breadth do not meet the letter of the Priestly Yardstick are sentenced to torture and prison. Their heinous crime was the heresy of daring to think and believe freely. It is into this world of ecclesiastical scourge and pious inquiry of condemnation that Christ chooses to return.

But what a strange thing! The Lord of the church does not appear to the ecclesiastical leaders of Seville. No. He comes to walk among the common people! He chooses not the *examiners* but the *suspects* for His visit!

In the marketplace He appears again. For some He brings word of encouragement, while for others He speaks conciliation. Once again the sick are healed and the lame walk. The common people have been made glad!

Quickly the word spreads to the Inquisitor General. With alarm he hears of the strange turn of events. It must not be! It must stop! The soldiers of the church are summoned. So with utter irony Jesus is arrested. Not

Caesar but the Church brings Christ to the dungeon to undergo judgment on His mission.

In the darkest hour of the night the inquisitor descends to the depths of the moldy jail to begin his examination. In contemptuous tones he probes Jesus' mind.

"What is this that you think you're doing? Why have you come here? Why have you come back? And this mingling with the common people, how dare you give them this freedom!

"Listen, Jesus, remember those stones which you were challenged to turn into bread? You said, 'Man does not live by bread alone, but by every word that proceeds from the mouth of God. Well, you were wrong. You should have turned stone into bread. Men need bread, not words that make them free. People have an agonizing time if they have to make free decisions.

"Therefore, the church has taken that freedom away. We have given people rules. We have taken that freedom away, and they love us for it. We no longer cause them the agony of having to freely decide. You must stay away. Do not give these people freedom again!"

With an ominous silence born of the ages, Jesus stands up. In utter simplicity He walks to the inquisitor. Bringing the warmth of His special embrace, He kisses this vicious priest on the cheek and just walks out. Nothing is said. There is only a quietness that hangs with the heaviness of final judgment in His quiet kiss.

Out of that solitude the words seem to float back from another time, from another marketplace, from another midnight prison: "If you mingle in my words, continue in my words, they will make you free anyway."

Man is not made to have his thoughts first digested by someone else. To be created in the image of God is to be made for freedom, and Jesus Christ came to accomplish this final liberation.

There are people who do not believe we ought to be free; they want to keep decisions secret and save us from the task of thinking for ourselves. At the other extreme, there are also people who believe that they do not have the ability to face themselves or to decide freely. They feel they can't stand up and be a whole person. To all of these "hesitators" Jesus comes and gives His same liberating kiss. He says, "I will make you free indeed."

The Greek meaning of the phrase "if you continue in my word" is "if you mingle and mix." It is a chewing, saturating, going-through process. Christ's words must sift and silt their way through all our being. Once they do, we are liberated people. And as liberated people we are able to face anything life has to give us.

Let's pursue the touch of Christ that comes from mixing in His Word. Let's look at how He would free us to be uniquely ourselves and His.

Why Split Your Personality?

Christ's first fingerprint of freedom unlocks self-deception. One of the roots of all emotional difficulty is the failure to recognize reality. So often the thing that ushers in other problems is simply our inability to face things the way they are; we prefer to deceive ourselves. Jesus comes to liberate us from this sin of self-deception.

I am using the word "sin" very advisedly. Sin by definition is anything that separates us from God, from other people, and from ourselves. Self-deception splits us off from each other, from God, and ultimately from ourselves. Christ develops people who do not have to live with these destructive illusions.

How is it that we become self-deceiving individuals? Something like this may happen in every person's life. We start childhood with no pretensions; we are whatever we are. However, we discover very quickly that when we are just ourselves, this isn't adequate for our parents! They tell us we have to be different.

"Don't do that! You know better! Don't pick your nose in public. That's bad." On and on it runs, from morning until night.

Keith Miller tells the story of a little child going into the department store and getting his finger caught in the door. The finger is torn and the nail is beginning to turn blue. He observes the mother saying, "Shut up, quit crying, you're creating a scene. It doesn't hurt." Blood drips from her child's finger, yet the embarrassed mother wants him to be quiet, to act as though nothing is wrong.

With this kind of childhood indoctrination we all learn quickly that the "real me" is not acceptable. There is another me that must be shown to the world.

I must have a plastered-on smile and keep saying that everything is always all right. The "I-never-feel-any-thing-bad" image is demanded of me or I am not accept-able to society. So I develop a "real self" and an "idealized self."

The real self is inside, filled with natural reactions, hopes, fears, doubts, and misgivings. The idealized self is an image developed to fit whatever seems appropriate for other people's expectations.

Then I go off to school. I pretty quickly discover that the teacher and the kids don't really like the real me, so I have to act in certain specified ways to feel like I am really "in."

The idealized self is now fully in operation, covering the true feelings with a veneer of social adaptation. The older I get and the more socially fluent I become, the more developed this facade becomes: Finally I really don't know if it's the real me or the mask I'm wearing that does the talking!

We see each other and say, "Gee, it's good to see you." Our real self is saying, "Oh no, not that oaf again!" The contrast is amazing.

"How are you feeling?"

"I'm feeling great."

The real self says, "I wish I was home in bed!" We are trapped behind the facade!

This develops until I reach the point where my own gifts aren't good enough. Just the ability to be myself isn't good enough. I feel I have to be something better than my true self. I no longer feel that I can just let my hair down and encounter others. I must put up another front. After a while I relate to others totally out of that phony front and lose my own ability to know what's really going on behind my own face.

Artificiality can be devastating in marriage. It creates enormous problems in how we relate and how we understand ourselves. We end up being very defeated by the deceptions with which we live.

Trick-or-Treat Christians

When we come to church we bring this whole mess with us before God. In this frame of mind we strain our prayers through these self-deceptions. The end result is that we ask God to baptize our illusions! We ask God to accomplish our deception. And then we wonder why our prayers aren't answered!

So often we think, "If God is going to inspire me and use me, He can't just use the real me. He's got to use some great facade that I put on." Fortunately, our God is the God of reality. He says, "I'm not about to baptize that Halloween job you're doing. I want you to be real."

This phoniness is entrenched in America's middle-class society. It has been characterized as the society of appearances. Our need to appear socially acceptable produces a shallowness that reduces conversation and personal encounters to banality. The youth of the 60's rose up to call a plague on this whole practice. Tragically, they came to feel that the whole church of the middle class was just one more projection of artificiality. Though this wasn't completely true, the kids were on to something.

Too often we gather with smiles that conceal broken, aching hearts. What we really need is the freedom to cry as well as to look great.

When I went to seminary half the guys wanted to be Billy Graham. In preaching class they would get up and proclaim, "The Bible says! " They even held their hands like Graham. (I always wanted to be a combination of Will Rogers and Peter Marshall.) We were all convinced that being ourselves was not enough for God. It had to be something artificial that we put on. When we carried this around with us, our relationships were depleted. Our experience of God was shallow and empty.

It is still incredible to me to consider the real way that God comes to us. I have heard Him saying to me, "If you are going to encounter me it must be on these terms. I like you as you are. My grace will encompass you as is. I want you to be what I uniquely have created you to be. I can't love people any other way!"

I struggle to believe the real gospel. It's too good to be true! For someone who grew up trying to be a "people pleaser" it's almost incomprehensible. I keep wanting to slip back to these old defeating patterns that are comfortable but phony. God's gracious love keeps pursuing, asking only to speak to the real Robert Wise. Sometimes it's not clear who that is. But His grace is persistent. He keeps asking, "Will the real Robert Wise please stand up?" When I do, God comes forth with an astonishing response that crams life full of utter reality!

131

The truth is that when I am busy trying to sell you my image and you are busy trying to sell me your image, we are in a game of trying to get each other to love phoniness. When I set artificiality aside, I can really love you, because it's just me encountering you. We can't do that until we are free.

It would be a conversion experience for many of us to decide to just be ourselves in the name of Christ. I am convinced that Jesus Christ is moving among us in His touching, loving way, wanting to make us free. He's still telling us, "We don't just live by bread alone. It's not enough to just get by, to live artificially. Your life is to be full, rich, free, and whole. That starts with you being the real you!"

Embrace Yourself!

Let's state this another way. So many of us find it easier to believe that God loves us than to believe we can love ourselves. It's a real turning point in a person's life to look at himself and realize that God does not make junk. Whatever He has made, He made intentionally. He wants me to embrace myself in the same way that He embraces me.

This isn't egotism. Inordinate preoccupation with self is more often born of doubt than of assurance. Much egotism is conquered when one develops a real appreciation of oneself "as is." To embrace myself as God embraces me releases me from all pretensions. It is enough to know that I am loved by Him and to dare to let that be.

This is where social deception begins to break up and vanish. It is enough "to be." My life finds its completion not in doing, acquiring, performing, or asserting, but in the simple fact that I *am*.

God is saying, "Stand up and be you! Cut out the

phony stuff—I can't use it! But I really can use what you were uniquely made to be."

But Life Is So Gray

I know it is easier to *describe* the Christ-style than to live it. Sometimes I'm not always sure who the real me is. Sometimes life doesn't come to me so simply that I can slice it into convenient compartments.

I am caught in duplicities and ambiguities. There are lots of grays and shadows. My best friends are not entirely honest and my worst enemies are never completely corrupt. At these confused times I reread a poem written by Dietrich Bonhoeffer. It helps me cut through the maze to the real center.

Bonhoeffer was one of our greatest twentieth-century theologians and martyrs for the Christian faith. Just before he was hanged in prison by the Nazis in 1945, Bonhoeffer wrote a little poem—Who Am I?—about the inner tension he felt between what he appeared to be and what he felt he was. Around him people were saying, "Dietrich, you're the man who is able to face this torture!" And yet within him he feared something quite different.

> They often tell me I step
>   from my self-confinement
> Calmly, cheerfully, firmly,
>   like a squire from his country house.
> Who am I?
> They often tell me
>   that I used to speak to my wardens
> Friendly, clearly,
>   as though it were mine to command.
> Who am I?
> They also tell me
>   I bore the days of misfortune

Equitably, smiling, proudly,
  like one accustomed to win.
Am I then really
  all that which other men tell of?
Or am I only what
  I know of myself?
Restless, longing,
  sick like a bird in a cage.
Struggling for breath as the hands
  were compressing my throat.
Yearning for colors, for flowers,
  for voices of birds,
Thirsting for words of kindness
  or neighborliness,
Tossing in expectation
  of great events,
Powerlessly yearning for friends
  at an infinite distance.
Weary, empty of praying,
  looking, making faint,
Ready to say farewell to it all.
Who am I? This or the other?
Am I one person today
  and tomorrow another?
Am I both at once,
  a hypocrite before others and
Before myself a contemptible,
  woebegone weakling?
Or is something within me
  beating on me, flaying disorder
From victory already achieved?
Who am I, why mock me,
  these lonely questions of mine?
Who am I? Thou knowest, O God,
  I am Thine.[2]

I am God's. It is when I have finally decided that my existence is His that I am free. I am thine, O Lord! Not the facade, not the image, but I am thine!

Our problem is that we try to "act" instead of learning to be who we are. Jesus Christ comes to give us that kiss that says, "If you will be mine, I will help you to be what you are." This is freedom from personal deception.

The Big Social Squeeze

Now what about freedom from social deception? How can I find freedom from the deceptions that are put upon me by my society? It is hard to live in a society of appearances. Romans says, "Don't let the world around you squeeze you into its own mold" (Rom. 12:2, *Phillips*). The truth is that every one of us lives with a tremendous struggle in the midst of a culture which is constantly pressuring us to be what that culture tells us is adequate, acceptable, etc. I am convinced that Jesus wants to free us from this social pressure.

In America we live in a performance-oriented society. We live in a society which tends to measure the worth of people by how much they produce. If they produce enough in both quantity and significance, they are really valuable. If they do not, they are not valuable. Society does not teach us to evaluate and value persons because they are people, but to evaluate them because of how they perform. Look at a couple of examples:

I grew up in a western Oklahoma town that is in the middle of a Cheyenne-Arapahoe Indian settlement. Whites in the entire area had a rather distinct attitude toward all Indians: they were of very limited value. Why? Because they produced so little!

If an Indian could make the football team, however, his whole status would change. Suddenly he had a great deal of worth. Simply being a human being who was at

135

peace with the prairie wasn't enough. An Indian had to meet white performance standards in order to qualify on the social scale.

Ivan Illyich, the gifted philosopher, talks about how we build this performance principle into our school system. Grade levels no longer indicate real educational achievement; instead they have come to signify rungs on the social ladder. You're not too much if you only reached a grade 8 level. However, if you went on to grade 16 (college graduate) you must be of value. Now, should you reach out beyond and go through all the steps to grade 20 (Ph.D.) you will have "total" social worth. Illyich notes that the result is destruction of much of the educational value in our school system. We produce a strange, distorted perspective on personal worth.

Consider another example. Why is it that many of us pass our middle years with such despair? For many of us this time is almost tantamount to disaster. When we reach the point where we see our productivity starting to wane, we find it difficult to live with ourselves. Why?

We didn't reach as high as we were supposed to, so we can't feel we're good enough. We're not as good as we could have been. Because our performance begins to decrease, something deep within begins to gnaw away at us. We feel as if we are empty people. In our performance-oriented society, we believe we are valuable only when we are significant producers.

While all this certainty isn't natural from a biblical viewpoint, we are all taught to accept it because "this is the way it is." Society does squeeze us into its mold, and the result is despair!

How to Be OK "As Is"

We preach that we are saved by grace through faith,

and not of ourselves (see Eph. 2:8). We've got to experience emotionally the amazing truth that no man can earn his way into the Kingdom of God. Salvation comes to us as a gift; no man earns his self-worth. There is *nothing* you can do to make yourself feel like you are really worthy. It is first and finally God's gift to you through faith. Only as you believe that God sees you as worthy already, and then accept what He has given you, that you can learn to live out of His measure of life rather than society's or anyone else's.

I am OK because God has found me to be OK. When I am unable to produce, He still finds me to be OK. When my life is all over and I've tied it all up, I don't know how the credits will read. But if I feel they are not enough, that's still all right, because Jesus Christ finds me to be His.

This is true not because of what I have accumulated or will ever accumulate, but purely by His grace and His love. It is only as I learn to evaluate my life through Him that I can be truly free. I am free of all of the phoniness! And that includes anyone else's evaluation!

When I know that I'm OK because of God's grace and not my performance, I will never worry again about the social register. I know that I will always be appropriately dressed. I will be OK.

And I can even admit my mistakes. The performance-oriented culture says it's wrong to ever be wrong. You don't have to be right. You don't have to win all the time. You can actually be wrong some of the time and it's OK!

I had a friend who used to call me on the phone on Monday mornings. I'd pick up the phone and this minister would say, "Hello, this is God. I have a gift for you today. I want to give you the gift of failing. Today you do not have to succeed. I grant that to you." Then he would hang up. I would sit there for 10 minutes staring at the wall.

The first time I couldn't believe it. It was really the gospel. God's love means it's even OK to fail. You don't have to be the greatest thing in the world. You can just be you. And that's OK. In God's name it's OK.

When you get rid of the personal fear and the social deception, a marvelous liberation comes over you. You are able to enjoy life in the real world. You can leave behind fantasized images that keep you operating in a fictionalized world you maintain in your head. God doesn't live in a make-believe universe. This is why we miss Him so much. We look for Him in an idealized world and go right past Him in everyday life. God's abode is in this creation of ambiguities, complexities, contradictions, and uncertainties. He lives with the worst and the best in you, but always it is with the real *you*. That's where God is, and that's why we miss Him so much. We look for Him in the idealized world, but we go right past Him here in the real world.

Jesus and Your Kitchen Table

Richard Nash wrote a bit of dialogue in "The Rainmaker" that catches this for me. In a secular vein it spells out an eternal truth. One central character is Starbuck, and he is a dreamer whose dreams never quite come true. He has complained about this to Liz, who knows how to live in reality.

He says to her, "Nothing's as pretty in your hands as it is in your head. There ain't no world as good as what I got up here. Know why that is?"

She replies, "I don't know, maybe it's because you don't have time to see it. You always have to run, to come, to go, maybe it helps you keep company with the world?"

Starbuck says, "You think I'd learn to love it?"

Liz answers, "Well, you might if you saw it real. Like some nights I'm in the kitchen washing dishes and Pop's playing poker with the guys. Well, I watch him real close and at first I just see an ordinary middle-aged man, not very interesting to look at, and then minute by minute I see little things I never noticed he had. Ways of talking I never paid any mind to. Suddenly, I know who he is and I love him so much I could cry. And I want to thank God I took time to see him real."[3]

Too many of us who are always running "out there" somewhere find that, all the time, life is right here. Fullness is in the real, the now. God would free us, Jesus Christ would liberate us, to the joy of the real. How do you get that here and now? How do you find that?

Well, it is not enough to just read what I've written so far. That's a start, but it's got to mingle and mix and saturate itself through you. The reason this doesn't happen for many of us is that we don't take the time to get into the real proximity to life as it comes by, and to Christ Himself.

Here's a little device that really helps me. I block out enough time each day in which I cannot be disturbed, in which I am totally alone.

When you are in solitude, sitting on a rock somewhere or at your kitchen table, away from distraction, take at least 15 minutes. For some people it could be 45 minutes to an hour. Start by deciding that you will do nothing but be absolutely quiet, that you will think about nothing. As you do this you will find in the center of your life a hollowed-out, quiet place. You are reaching into the absolute center of your being. Do nothing. Think about nothing. Just sit there. It is like letting mud and silt precipitate out of muddy water till it's clear.

During the first five minutes of quietness you'll think, "Boy, is this crazy! This is dumb! This is ridiculous!"

Probably during the second five to ten minutes you'll think, "How do you stop thinking about thinking? How do I quiet my mind?"

But just keep on! Let the old pressures keep bouncing around. They will ricochet less and less, until finally you are truly silent at the center. Maybe for the first time you will enter your churning place without apprehension. In quietness and confidence look around and observe the dimensions of your cares and fears. As the dust settles in this silent chamber, walk along the floor and study the strange aberrations that rest there, waiting only for your anxieties and misdirected emotions to bring them back to frantic flight. Note carefully what feeds them and what might put them to death. Come to know your churning place from the inside.

Then in that quietness of the absolute center of your being, begin to pray, "Lord Jesus Christ, free me, take away my mask, take away my fears, take away my apprehensions by which I live and let the real me come forth."

Keep pursuing this prayer, asking the Holy Spirit to really free you and loosen you. Listen long enough, and soon you will hear the squeak of sandals and the swish of robes. Wait until Christ kisses you on the cheek. Only then will you discover that you have become truly liberated. Only then will you find true peace in your churning place.

Some Helps to Wholeness

As the requests of this prayer become the desires of your heart, you will enter into new wholeness and freedom in your life. Remember, those who "hunger and thirst after righteousness" will be satisfied.

Gracious heavenly Father, we would find you walking in our midst. Touch us at whatever point it is necessary. We would linger long enough to let you push our emotions back. Free us from the phony, the artificial roles put upon us by society. Liberate us from the needs created out of our past. We long to be authentically yours. Free us to live without fear, deception, anxiety, and self-centeredness. Allow us to love ourselves as you love us, to love others as we are intended to love them, and in all things to let you be the Refiner of our personhood, to know that we are finally yours. In Christ's name. Amen.

For Further Consideration

1. What does it really mean for you to be free, to be liberated? What are the dangers in freedom? What are the possibilities?

2. Honestly, how do you deceive yourself? Do you laugh when you want to cry? Do you say yes when you want to say no? Do you smile when you really hurt?

3. How do you let social pressure press you into someone else's image? Do you let social expectations rob you of the joy of being who you truly are?

4. Do you know that Jesus Christ has also given you the right to fail?

5. If Christ would return physically, as in the story of the Grand Inquisitor, what could He do for you per-

sonally Write it down. If you believe this is true and realistic, why not set out on your own spiritual pilgrimage to realize the gift?

Footnotes

1. Fyodor M. Dostoyevsky, *The Brothers Karamozov,* Great Books of the Western World (Chicago: Encyclopedia Britanncia Inc., 1952) pp. 127-137.
2. Dietrich Bonhoeffer, *The Cost of Discipleship* (New York: The Macmillan Co., 1963). pp. 18-20.
3. N. Richard Nash, "The Rainmaker," *Harper's Magazine,* 1955.